INFLATION, POORTALK, and the GOSPEL

THOMAS E. LUDWIG **MEROLD WESTPHAL** **ROBIN KLAY** **DAVID G. MYERS**

Judson Press ® Valley Forge

INFLATION, POORTALK, AND THE GOSPEL

Library of Congress Cataloging in Publication Data

Main entry under title:

Inflation, poortalk, and the Gospel.

  Includes bibliographical references and index.
  1. Finance, Personal. 2. Inflation (Finance)
3. Christianity and economics. I. Ludwig, Thomas E.
HG179.I486   332.024'02   81-8248
ISBN 0-8170-0942-6   AACR2

Contents

Preface

Some books ask to be written. This is one of them. Its genesis occurred when Dave Myers, weary of commiserating "poortalk" by middle-class folk, pondered how certain principles from psychological research might explain people's economic frustrations amidst rising affluence. Dave shared his thoughts with me and together we organized them into a magazine piece.

The resulting article ("Let's Cut the Poortalk," *Saturday Review*, October 28, 1978) and a companion piece ("How Christians Can Cope with Inflation," *Christian Century*, May 30, 1979) evoked many responses, among which was an invitation to write this book.

As research psychologists we could speak with but limited authority on economic and philosophical/theological matters. So we obtained the collaboration of two friends, Robin Klay, an economist with experience in Third World countries, and Merold Westphal, a philosopher experienced in conducting workshops on simple living and the global future.

After formulating the book's organization, we each drafted chapters in our areas of competence. We then discussed each chapter and edited the manuscript to a more unified style.

The resulting book has benefited from critiques by several of our friends—Carol Myers, Barrie Richardson, Gerard Van Heest, and Carol Westphal. Karen Alderink's professional manuscript preparation skills greatly facilitated the editing of successive drafts. To Hope College, which supported our collaboration with a faculty grant, and to each one of these people, we owe our thanks.

Tom Ludwig—January, 1981

Introduction

What Is the Problem?

The uncertainties of our time have generated as much inflation in rhetoric and doomsaying as in prices. Economic "thrillers" such as Howard Ruff's *How to Prosper During the Coming Bad Years* have sent some people scurrying for cover, expecting the sky to fall. The news media assail us with daily reports of high inflation, rising taxes, and persistent unemployment. Respected public figures are beginning to wonder whether the "good old days" of American prosperity are almost over. And even if our rising prosperity continues, some people question how long the natural environment can sustain economic growth.

No wonder Americans are worried and frustrated. The easy answers and quick solutions we have come to expect are no longer available. In one sense this is fortunate, for it prompts us to take a hard look at the personal and national issues confronting us.

During this period of our history Christians have two reasons to be informed and active: On the one hand, the economic pressures in our society may be working against the biblical norms of justice and charity. On the other hand, Christians may be in a unique position to serve as models of successful adaptation to the new economic realities.

To help Christians meet these challenges, we have brought together insights from economics, psychology, philosophy, and biblical theology to answer two questions: (1) What impact does the current economic situation have on us as individuals and on our world? (2) How might Christians respond to the situation in ways that are both biblically sound and beneficial to themselves and other people?

Plan of the Book

Chapter 1 examines the personal financial impact of inflation and related economic ailments. Who suffers most from inflation? Do the rich get richer and the poor get poorer? You will find some answers here.

Chapter 2 describes the present state of our economy and how it got that way. We will see that while the complex pattern of inflation, slow productivity growth, and high energy prices warrants analysis and action, it does not call for national panic or a "grab-it-while-you-can" personal response.

Chapter 3 analyzes the psychological impact of inflation. We will examine a number of psychological forces that combine to make us feel worse than necessary about our economic situation.

The net result of these economic and psychological pressures is a temptation to turn inward, focusing so intently on our own pocketbooks that we are blinded to the needs of others. But Christians who understand these economic and psychological forces will realize the need for personal and societal action. Where do we turn for help in choosing responsible and appropriate actions? Chapter 4 offers biblical guidelines.

Chapter 5 applies those guidelines to our attitudes and provides suggestions for changing the way we think about possessions, about happiness, and about success.

Chapter 6 explores the implications of the biblical guidelines for our behavior now. We can do some things to free ourselves from grasping consumerism and to reach out to those whose needs are greater than ours.

Biblical principles apply in times of prosperity and in times of economic adversity. Chapter 7 spins out optimistic and pessimistic visions of our economic future and discusses ways in which Christians could live responsibly in each of these settings.

Finally, chapter 8 reminds us why we can live lives of joyful celebration as we work for a more just society.

People in the Pinch

Part 1

1

How Does
Inflation Hit Us?

We are living in a difficult period. Across the country, people are feeling the pinch of persistent inflation. The talk is of cutting back, retrenching, trimming budgets; all around us economic conditions are causing physical hardship and emotional stress. But economic changes seldom affect everyone equally. Inflation is a case in point: While some people suffer from inflation, others actually profit from it.

Who Are the Winners and Losers?
Personal Income

One way to see who is winning and who is losing the battle with inflation is to look at changes in the buying power of different occupational groups over the last decade.[1] From 1967 to 1978 the cost of living doubled; that is, the consumer price index went up 100 percent. The rising incomes of some groups—police officers, physicians, and construction workers—have almost exactly matched the rise in prices. Other groups, such as unionized factory workers and truck drivers, have managed to raise their incomes substantially faster than inflation. Steelworkers' pay went up 165 percent; autoworkers', 146 percent; and truckers', 122 percent.

Who, then, are the losers? In terms of income growth, certain professional and occupational groups have clearly lost ground. Librarians' income rose only 63 percent, while college professors, with a 76 percent increase, have also fallen behind. Even United States senators with 1978 salaries of $57,000 plus expenses managed to raise their incomes only 90 percent.

Welfare recipients have also been losers. While living costs were doubling, their average benefits rose only 62 percent. Other groups receiving checks from government treasuries have done much better. The average Social Security benefit rose 210 percent between 1967 and 1978.[2] Retirees on military and federal civil service pensions also made substantial gains. Although federal pensions were once relatively low, now, according to benefits specialist Arch Patton, upper-level federal employees who retired at age sixty-five in 1970 are receiving pensions almost double the combined totals of pension and Social Security benefits for nongovernment workers.[3] But government clerks and secretaries are worse off now than in 1967.[4] Their incomes have increased only 89 percent in contrast to the 113 percent their bosses have received.

Of course, no one would argue that the relative wage structure in 1967 was fair to all occupational groups. Indeed, it is possible that some of the relative changes since then may have compensated for past economic imbalances. For example, coal miners working in hazardous conditions may have deserved their 158 percent increase in pay. But on the whole the societal adjustment to inflation has redistributed wealth from less powerful individuals (e.g., non-unionized librarians) to highly organized and powerful occupational groups.

Total Assets

Inflation's impact can also be seen in changes in the real value of assets for each economic class in our society. Joseph Minarik of the Brookings Institute argues that, proportionately, those who "suffer" most from inflation are the wealthy.[5] Wealthy individuals tend to have more of their assets in stocks and bonds. Since stock prices tend to decline during high inflation, the real value of many paper fortunes has dropped considerably. For example, although the dollar value of Harvard University's endowment rose 34 percent between 1967 and 1978, each of those dollars is now worth less than half a 1967 dollar. Thus, the real value of Harvard's assets declined by a third.

Minarik claims that, in terms of total assets, middle-class homeowners have profited most from the years of inflation, because the value of their homes has risen faster than inflation. Moreover, each year of inflation decreases the percentage of their total income that must be set aside for their fixed mortgage payment. The $112-a-month mortgage that one of the authors began paying in 1969 was a 20 percent bite of his monthly take-home pay then; today it is but a 7 percent nibble.

But this is only part of the story. On the one hand, it is difficult to feel pity for the millionaires whose assets have dropped in real value. They may feel the loss, but their remaining wealth is sufficient to cushion inflation's impact. On the other hand, even though the real income of some poor people has kept pace with inflation, the poor are especially hurt whenever the cost of basic necessities such as food, housing, and heat rises faster than overall inflation. The poor can least afford these increases because their disposable income is less "disposable"; a higher proportion of it was already going to such expenses, leaving less surplus to absorb the increases. In cities where strong rent control policies have slowed the rise in housing costs for the poor, a new crisis has developed: Landlords are converting their apartment buildings into condominiums or abandoning them, thus turning the problem of cost into one of unavailability.

Inflation's Impact on Opportunities

It is a truism that inflation hurts people on low fixed incomes. But inflation does more than merely sap their buying power; it has an insidious effect on the opportunities open to them. For years the standard of living for the poor had been increasing as a result of the "trickle-down effect": the expanding economic "pie" meant new jobs for some of the poor and new social programs for others, without decreasing the share of the pie that other groups received. But the combination of rapid inflation and slow economic growth has kept the pie from expanding. At least for the next several years, argues economist Lester Thurow, we will be in a "zero-sum" economy; every gain in income or opportunities by one group will mean a corresponding loss by some other group.[6]

Inflation also undermines opportunities for the poor by weakening public education. The cost of everything from textbooks and supplies to teachers' salaries is rising rapidly while inflation-burdened taxpayers vote down millage increases and threaten to cut existing revenues. As the quality of the public schools declines (beginning with the loss of such "luxuries" as art and music programs), middle-class parents transfer their children to private schools. Since those parents are now even less likely to vote for increased school taxes, the quality of education drops even further. The loss of some of the bright, motivated students lowers teacher morale and the opportunities for academic competition. As Fred Hechinger argues, "Eventually the public schools will be left with only the poorest and the most deprived, as they were before the process of educational democratization began a century ago. More is involved: At stake is the difference between a fluid and a stratified society."[7]

Inflation's Impact on Our Taxes
Federal Taxes

The federal income tax is "progressive" in the sense that people with higher incomes pay a higher proportion of their incomes in taxes than do people with lower incomes. This means that inflation can directly increase our income tax burden through "tax-bracket creep." If the cost of living goes up 8 percent and our salary also increases by 8 percent, we may actually lose because our income taxes will increase more than 8 percent if we move into a higher tax bracket.

Some economists refer to the increased revenue generated by bracket creep as "windfall taxes," or as government's "inflation dividend," since our elected representatives did not have to vote for an increase in tax rates. "Why should the government gain from inflation while the rest of us lose?" question many economists. They propose that tax rates be "indexed" to price increases so that wage increases that merely compensate for inflation would not cause an individual's tax burden to rise as well.[8]

Other economists argue that the problem is less severe than it

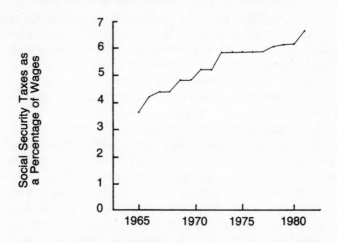

Figure 1.1. Higher Social Security Benefits + more retirees = higher payroll taxes.

appears, because tax reforms enacted over the past two decades have compensated for bracket creep for many people; thus, the total tax revenues of the federal government actually have *not* increased substantially.[9] However, the tax breaks engineered through this political system have not benefited everyone equally; in general, the reforms have eased the tax burden of the poor and the very rich, but have done little to help middle-income families.

Inflation's impact on the Social Security payroll tax has been substantial (see Figure 1.1). If the amount contributed by the employer is also considered, the total tax constitutes over 12 percent of earnings, our largest single tax. Since Social Security benefits are now indexed to the rate of inflation, each rise in the consumer price index brings a corresponding increase in benefits, thus assuring further increases in the payroll tax on today's workers. The problem is compounded by the fact that our society is growing older; the number of people drawing Social Security benefits is growing much

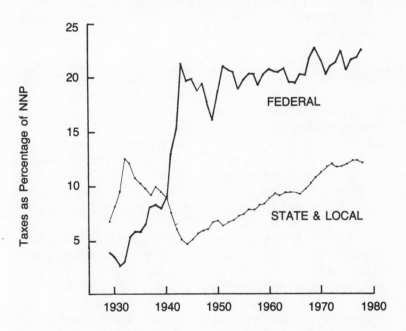

FIGURE 1.2. Tax receipts as a percentage of net national product (gross national product less capital consumption allowances).

faster than the number of workers. As proportionately fewer workers fund benefits for more and more retirees, the payroll tax burden will grow.

State and Local Taxes

But even with "bracket creep" and increased Social Security taxes, the total tax burden the federal government imposed on us grew rather slowly over the 1970s. Why, then, are Americans so upset about taxes? The answer seems to lie in the rapidly increasing burden of state and local taxes,[10] which have risen faster than federal taxes in recent years (see Figure 1.2). Also, in contrast to federal taxes, which are silently deducted from our paychecks, local taxes are highly visible. They are added to the cost of our purchases or must be paid in cash at city hall. The federal income tax is progressive, but most local property taxes do not reflect the individual's ability to pay, nor are they closely related to the benefits (such as fire and police protection) received by the property owners. Furthermore, increased house values are for most homeowners merely a paper profit, the actual effect of which is to create higher property taxes.

Inflation's Impact on Morale and Morality

Inflation in the 1970s took a toll on the average person's psychological well-being. Ironically, the emotional toll far exceeded the actual economic changes. Even though, objectively speaking, middle-class individuals (especially homeowners) have "suffered" less from inflation than other groups, findings from national surveys indicate that the middle class *feels* most adversely affected. The middle class seems to believe that the poor are well served by government assistance, while the rich have sufficient assets and tax advantages to profit regardless of the economic climate.

A pair of surveys conducted in 1976 and 1978 by Avraham Shama lends support to this notion.[11] Contrary to conventional wisdom and liberal economic theory, the young, professional, educated, white, moderately affluent people felt hurt the worst. Apparently the years of prosperity convinced these people that rapidly rising affluence was their birthright; when they were forced to cut back, their high expectations made them feel the sharpest loss. The poor seem to feel less hurt by inflation because the American dream was never as real to them.

The low morale of the middle class may also be due to

economic uncertainties. According to Richard Curtin of the University of Michigan Survey Research Center, sharply fluctuating wages and prices make people feel insecure and make it hard for them to plan for the future.[12] People wonder, "How can we save for our children's education or our retirement when we don't even know how much money we'll need then?" Uncertainty postpones the necessary adjustments to the new economic realities and thus prolongs the psychological trauma. The poor may feel this trauma less, because they experience less uncertainty. Since they have few assets, the highly variable yields from investments do not affect their future plans.

FIGURE 1.3. Rapid inflation puts us into a race with prices. This can lead to lower morale and greater uncertainty about the future.

Drawing by Geo. Price; © 1972 The New Yorker Magazine, Inc.

Inflation also has an impact on the middle class's perception of independence and freedom of choice. Middle-class people used to feel more in control of their lives and more able to manipulate the environment to get what they wanted. Good, hard work brought guaranteed rewards. Planning for the future is a classic middle-class preoccupation, made possible by the sense of security that prosperity brings.

Inflation has weakened this sense of control. "I don't know what's going to happen next week, let alone next year," complains a Boston carpenter. "It doesn't seem to matter how hard you work anymore; you can't keep up with these prices." A California couple moans, "It seems like we're always having to work harder and

harder just to stay where we are." The traditional qualities of
integrity and hard work no longer produce guaranteed affluence.
Many people believe that saving money, the traditional means of
increasing one's future options, no longer makes sense. As F.
Harvey Popell argues, "Why save for a rainy day when one's savings
won't buy an umbrella when needed? . . . Why be scrupulously
honest and keep one's shoulder to the wheel seeking long-term
personal growth when there is no long term on the horizon?"[13]

An outgrowth of this loss of control is to shorten our horizons
for making plans. The uncertainty about prices next year leads
people to spend now. The uncertainty about future yields leads
investors to channel funds into inflation hedges rather than
productive investments. This phenomenon of shortened horizons
may be new for the middle class, but the poor have been
experiencing it all along as one aspect of the cycle of poverty. The
poor have literally been forced to eat their planting seed or burn
their cabin floorboards to survive today rather than plan for
tomorrow.

Inflation may be eroding our morality as well as our morale.
The middle-class perception that we are simultaneously being
cheated out of our deserved prosperity and losing control over our
future has implications for generosity and charitable contributions.
As middle-class families see themselves drowning in a pool of red
ink, they may justify keeping a tighter grip on their purse strings.
The tax-revolt fever that has swept the country illustrates the
decreased willingness of people in the pinch to bear one another's
economic burdens.

All of us are feeling inflation's squeeze. We see it at work, at
the supermarket, at the gas pump, at the car dealership. But to
understand *why* we are in inflation's grasp, we need to look at the
broader economic forces that cause inflation.

Questions for Further Consideration

1. Has inflation eroded your family's standard of living? If so, in
   what specific ways have you been forced to cut back? How do
   you feel about those changes? What impact has inflation had on
   the churches, schools, and other organizations in your
   community?
2. Is the present distribution of wealth in our country just? Do the
   incomes of the various occupational groups reflect their

contributions to society? What, if anything, should our society be doing to ease the burden on those who have been hurt most by inflation?

3. Inflation provokes us to question the prudence of the traditional virtues of saving money, hard work, and honesty. What are the implications for us as individuals and for society?

4. What would happen if economic stagnation became permanent? Should some people be forced to accept a smaller slice of the income "pie" or the opportunities "pie" so that others can have a larger share? Would you be willing to make such a sacrifice?

5. Have you responded to inflation by choosing to reduce your charitable contributions, either in dollar amounts or as a percentage of your income? If times get worse, do you think Americans will draw together and dig more deeply to help one another? Or will they become more concerned with their own financial survival and less open to the needs of others?

6. Why do all of us, including those who are net gainers in inflationary periods, *feel* hurt by inflation?

2

How Did We Get into This Mess?

What Has Gone Wrong?*

How did we get into this "mess"? Why has the American dream of ever-increasing prosperity lost its luster for many people? What could have prompted Federal Reserve Board Chairman Paul Volcker to predict that "the American standard of living [has] to decline"?[1]

Simplistic Answers

Are our problems the result of high taxes? Many of those who read the current economic situation as a "crisis leading to disaster" blame the increasing burden of government. But neither historical trends nor international comparisons support this simple diagnosis.

Since World War II, the share of the American gross national product going to finance all levels of government has indeed risen slowly but steadily to about 30 percent of our national income. However, since the upward trend existed prior to recent slower economic growth, tax increases alone cannot explain our economy's current doldrums. Our taxes may seem high, but, except for Japan, they are the lowest among the major Western industrialized nations (see Figure 2.1). Not only is the financial burden of government in the United States comparatively light, but it also remained relatively constant during the 1970s, while the burden in most other

*This chapter presents a simplified analysis of the economic situation. At points we felt the need to make qualifying statements or to alert the reader to some of the complexities in the situation. Where we felt these parenthetical comments would confuse the reader or detract from the flow of the analysis, we placed our comments in the notes at the end of the book. The economic statistics on which we based our analysis can be found in *Historical Statistics of the United States* and *Statistical Abstract of the United States*.

countries markedly increased. For instance, in Sweden the share of tax revenues rose from 41 percent to *over half* of total income between 1970 and 1976.[2]

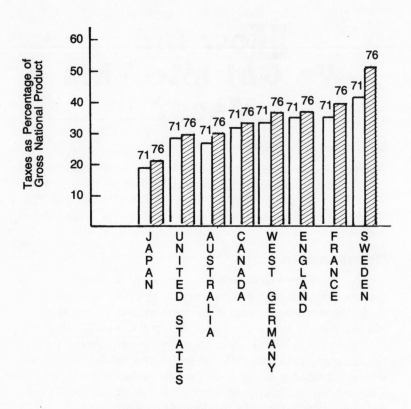

FIGURE 2.1. Tax revenues in relation to gross national product.

Are our problems caused by the welfare burden? Given the relatively mild increase in the proportion of our national income going to taxes, it makes little sense to suggest that our economic woes are caused by rising welfare rolls. Family incomes in this country are unequally distributed both before and after taxes. The poorest 30 percent of the American population receives (after taxes and income redistribution) only 9 percent of total national income. Among Western industrialized nations, only in France are the poor so much worse off than the rich. And the equalizing power of the United States tax and welfare system is no more than average when compared with other countries. Granted, all industrialized countries may be suffering slower economic growth because of income redistribution via the tax and welfare system.[3] But since taxing the affluent to provide for the poor is not new, it cannot account for the extent of our recent economic ailments.

So what is wrong with the economy? Economists believe our basic problem is that inflation has become deeply ingrained in our economy at the same time that we are experiencing a drop in the growth of productivity. When inflation and slow growth are combined with uncertainties in the price and availability of energy, we all feel the pinch.

Inflation—A Complex Problem

The 1980s began with a painful recession. Recession is not new. What is new is the recent experience of high and accelerating rates of inflation coupled with sluggish economic growth. Inflation (as measured by the consumer price index) averaged an annual 6.7 percent in the nation during the 1970s. In contrast, during the 1950s and 1960s, prices inched up at an average of less than 2 percent per

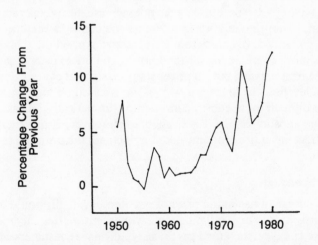

FIGURE 2.2. Year-to-year changes in the consumer price index illustrate inflation's accelerating pace.

year (see Figure 2.2). This new inflation is a worldwide problem. The only major Western industrialized country with lower inflation during the 1970s was Germany, with an average inflation rate of 5.6 percent. In Japan, inflation averaged 9.8 percent.

Economists now speak of prices "ratcheting upward." It used to be that economic downturns sufficiently cooled off the economy to reduce inflation. Prior to the 1930s, inflation alternated with periods of deflation in which prices sank as far as they had previously risen. But despite occasional recessions, the general price level has not gone down since the 1930s. Recent recessions have done no more than slow the pace of inflation; when business improved during the subsequent upswings, inflation moved upward from where it had leveled off.

What causes inflation? Why will it not go away? Economists disagree about the relative importance of any one cause, but they agree that inflation results from many interrelated factors.

External Shocks

Outside shocks to our economy, such as price hikes in imported raw materials, can initiate inflationary spurts. In earlier periods such price jolts did not generate sustained, economy-wide inflation. Changes in the prices of certain goods merely led buyers away from more expensive items to less expensive ones. Such adjustments were at times painful to consumers and to those left jobless by the shift in buying patterns, but they did not increase the overall rate of inflation. Today the situation is different. The main external shocks to the economy have come from a steady string of oil price hikes. When shortages create higher food prices, the prices usually drop after the next harvest, but oil prices show no signs of coming down or even leveling off. Since our way of life is based on high energy use, it is difficult to cut energy consumption dramatically, and as yet no cheap substitute for oil is available. Moreover, rising energy costs affect the entire economy and thus increase the overall rate of inflation.

Deficit Spending

Of course, a rise in the price of one item, even oil, would not necessarily lead to high inflation *if everyone were on fixed incomes.* On a fixed income, increased gas prices would leave consumers with no choice but to drive less or buy fewer steaks or other goods. Paying more for one item would mean buying less of other items; overall demand would drop enough to prevent overall inflation from rising rapidly. But in our example, that would mean harder times for farmers or layoffs for auto workers. Such adjustments can be socially wrenching; so modern governments have used the devices of easy credit and increased public spending to provide the additional buying power required to sustain earlier purchasing patterns.[4] This deficit spending contributes to inflation.

Inflationary Psychology

In the late sixties and early seventies many observers concluded that inflation was a cost worth paying to protect employment. Lately, however, inflation has become so painful that most observers now conclude that the cost is too high. As we bought off unemployment we created an inflation that generated expectations of further increases in prices and wages—all financed by liberal money policies and deficit spending. In the past consumers tended to respond to a rise in the cost of living by increasing savings and reducing consumption. And when people are not buying, prices stop rising. In 1979, however, consumers reacted to a decrease in the purchasing power of their earnings by spending *more* and saving less. This accelerated the rate of inflation.

Furthermore, workers once were presumed subject to "monetary illusion"; that is, they misperceived a rise in wage rates as an improvement, even though prices rose, too. If this ever was true of workers, it seems no longer to hold during periods of rapid inflation. Workers who bargain for wage increases, managers who set prices, and institutions that finance spending by both parties increasingly incorporate into their contracts expectations of high and rising inflation. Most of us want new contracts that will compensate for future as well as past inflation. When participants in the economy compete to protect their share of the inflated pie, an initially low rate of inflation can accelerate. This seems, indeed, to be what has happened in recent years. Now that 60 percent of American workers are partially protected by cost-of-living escalators in their contracts, inflation is chasing its own tail.

Borrow and Buy

Several attention-getting best-sellers are promising riches, or at least some financial security, to those who bet on inflation. One book cover proclaims that all we need do is invert the old "A penny saved is a penny earned" wisdom. The advice is "borrow and buy," since lenders and savers always lose during inflation. We are advised to purchase durables, collectibles, and precious metals.

Is this good advice? From an economic standpoint, our political and economic institutions may now be generating the will and the mechanisms to halt rapid inflation. If so, those who follow popular advice about how to invest in inflation will lose relative to those who put their money into more productive investments. Thus, those who put all their savings plus additional costly financing into the housing market or gold may end up worse off when houses do not sell or gold prices fall from an inflated high.

Can we stop inflation? Escalating inflation will continue unless our expectations of future price rises can be altered. If everyone anticipates high and rising inflation, they will act in ways that make the prophecy self-fulfilling. When everyone borrows and spends *now* in the expectation that prices will continue to rise, the tide cannot be easily checked *unless* government restricts the money available for borrowing and spending.

This is the position that most economic policymakers are now adopting. As this book was being written in the summer of 1980, housing prices (which increased 10.9 percent yearly between 1975 and 1979) met a lull. The lull was a direct result of a more restrictive money policy and credit controls. Since durable assets such as housing and precious metals are the scene of intense speculative fever in an inflationary economy, we may be seeing the first signs of a break in inflationary psychology. If some of those who literally banked on rising prices start to lose, then people will hesitate to speculate in ways that aggravate inflation; and some of those who bet on *falling* prices will now come out ahead of those who bet on inflation. It is easy to see why people resort to an individualistic, "looking out for Number One" strategy when they feel threatened by the economic future. It makes sense for all of us to try to maximize our gains and minimize our losses. But our individual gains may have broader social consequences. For example, if there is a rush to buy gold and silver, we will wind up wastefully devoting resources to their storage and protection, while diverting savings from more productive investments in industry.

What about barter? Both today and in the past some people have sought refuge from an unstable monetary system by resorting to barter. Doctors, lawyers, and plumbers agree to pay for one another's services by swapping. While this may protect the interest of some swappers, others lose when they cannot find high-quality services they wish to "purchase" in spite of the high demand for their own services. Also, barter constitutes a reversal of hard-won economic progress over the centuries whereby money facilitated the movement of surpluses over large distances to fill shortages. Thus, the results of barter could actually be an increase in inflation by reducing output.

Neither barter nor investments in precious metals is an adequate solution for inflation. If we all attempted to follow currently popular advice on how to beat inflation, the result could be much worse inflation.

Productivity—Inflation's Counterweight

Productivity is a measure of an economy's strength and the chief source of rising material welfare for any population. In the twenty-five years after World War II, American worker productivity (output per worker-hour) increased at about 3 percent a year. Over the 1970s, the annual productivity gain dwindled to about 1.5 percent.[5] This shrinking growth in productivity intensifies the inflation problem. If productivity were increasing rapidly, then producers would not have to pass on to consumers such a large share of increased costs of materials and labor.[6] Therefore, one way to fight inflation is to raise productivity.

Why Has Productivity Growth Slowed?

What is causing the productivity problem? Is it growth in the power of unions? No, the relative number of workers unionized has actually dropped slightly, from 23 percent in 1950 to 21 percent in the late 1970s. Is it lack of worker discipline? Contrary to popular belief, it has not been demonstrated that overall discipline and attitudes toward work were significantly worse in the latter half of the seventies than in earlier periods. The chief determinants of productivity growth have always been improvements not in the workers' attitudes but in the equipment they use and in their training and education.

So where lies the problem? Is it simply that pollution-control and safety requirements sap funds that would otherwise be invested in new manufacturing equipment? That may be part of the problem, but that burden has actually declined in recent years from 5.8 percent of total investment in 1975 to 4.3 percent in 1979.[7] Has productivity dropped because less money is being spent on research and development (R & D) of new, more labor-efficient machines and processes? Apparently not. Although the share of the United States gross national product spent on R & D has declined, this decline was limited to the public sector; R & D expenditures have not fallen in private industry. Consequently, none of the possibilities—unionization, worker laziness, safety and pollution-control costs, decreased R & D—satisfactorily explain the recent decline in productivity growth.

Shortened Horizons

A more likely explanation of the productivity problem is the combined effect of environmental and safety laws plus inflation itself. Swiftly rising, highly variable prices reduce productivity growth by promoting investment in shorter-lived assets. However, these investments (such as new equipment that uses no technological advances) generally contribute less to productivity than do longer-lived assets (such as industrial complexes using new technologies and producing for new markets). This emphasis on the short run is accentuated when environmental and safety requirements are becoming stricter. For instance, chemical companies may hesitate to expand for fear that their currently up-to-date waste disposal systems may later be judged criminally inadequate. Why commit ourselves to long-term investments if inflation, new regulations, and increased legal liabilities are likely to diminish the prospects for a good return? With these uncertainties, it is understandable that both producers and consumers prefer to operate within a short time horizon over which changes are more predictable and manageable.

There are other explanations for declining productivity: (1) the increased share of young, inexperienced workers (the "baby boom" generation) in the labor force; (2) a gradual shift in consumer spending from manufactured goods to services such as medical care in which productivity gains are harder to come by; (3) skyrocketing oil prices that have led businesses to invest more in increased energy efficiency than in increased labor productivity.

Of course, part of the "productivity problem" may be one of definition. Productivity statistics reflect increases in *marketed* output per worker-hour, not improvements in worker safety or in air and water quality. If environmental and safety concerns have lowered productivity growth as traditionally measured, perhaps that is a cost we should bear gladly.[8]

Why Us? Some Perspectives

Although we clearly have a problem, our economic condition does not warrant a national panic. A moment's reflection on comparisons with earlier generations and with other countries may convince us that now is not the time for a retreat into isolationism.

Are We Really "Suffering" More than in the Past?

Over the entire period between 1950 and 1980, disposable (after inflation and taxes) incomes per person were rising at an average of about 2.2 percent per year (see Figure 2.3). However, during the late 1970's incomes grew only 1.4 percent per year and actually fell slightly in 1980. If this lower growth were to persist, disposable incomes would double only every fifty years instead of every thirty-two years; so in one sense we are not doing as well. But in another sense we are suffering very little. The average American is still at or very close to the highest peak of affluence attained in our history.[9] The yelps of agony over the 1980 loss in buying power are,

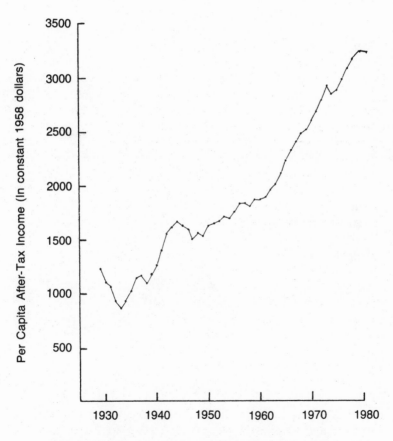

FIGURE 2.3. America's rising prosperity: disposable income per person (adjusted for taxes and inflation).

Figure 2.4. Inflation's impact.

in the historical perspective portrayed in Figure 2.3, "much ado about nothing." In spite of inflation, the economy has showered dollars on the average person faster than it has robbed those dollars of value.

Are We "Suffering" More than Other Industrialized Nations?

Many people believe that the United States once enjoyed a much higher growth rate than other industrialized countries and that now it is falling inexorably behind, perhaps because American workers are sloughing off when compared to still disciplined German and Japanese workers. Again, a quick look at the historical facts does not support this impression. During a whole century beginning in 1870, growth rates (in per capita GNP) were highly similar for the United States, Germany, France, Italy, and Canada. Thus, our country did *not* experience exceptional growth. Nor is it now alone in experiencing a decline in growth. During the seventies, even Japan's rate of growth fell to 3.8 percent (compared to 9.9 percent in the sixties). Growth rates in *all* industrialized countries have recently slowed.

Are We "Suffering" More than the Developing Nations?

Some suggest that chronic high inflation and economic stagnation are inevitable in mature industrial societies on the brink of deterioration. But our economic ills have not been balanced by boundless prosperity in less developed or newly industrialized nations. In spite of some remarkable increases in productivity and some sharply declining birthrates, many Third World economies are losing ground. Trapped between skyrocketing energy costs and inflated prices on goods imported from the West, they are forced to use scarce capital to pay foreign bills rather than expand their own industrial and food production.

Then Why All the Fuss?

The American economy is clearly facing some serious problems. But our perceived suffering is way out of proportion with our actual deprivations. The media may have contributed to our panic by showing us, week after week, shoppers recoiling in horror from the price tags on their purchases. The government's consumer price index may have contributed to our perceptions by overestimating inflation's impact on the average family, since most families do not buy a house or car every year and most families have substituted less expensive but equally satisfying goods for the products whose prices have inflated the fastest. The legions of doomsayers may have contributed by misreading cyclical fluctuations in the economy as signs of impending disaster.

Regardless of the reasons for our economic masochism, the fact remains that we are feeling the pinch. What will happen if things get worse? The possibility exists that *real* suffering could increase, both in the United States and around the world. How would we respond? To answer that question we need first to examine the ways in which inflation affects our emotions and our expectations for the future.

Questions for Further Consideration

1. There is nothing new about self-interested behavior. Harnessed in the right way, it can provide needed incentives for productive activity that serves all of society. But self-interest can turn from a social servant into a destabilizing force. How does inflation contribute to this process?
2. Why do so many people have the impression that we in the United States have worse inflation and lower productivity than the rest of the world?
3. Why do we find the simplest diagnosis of our economic difficulties (for instance, high taxes, OPEC prices, irresponsible unions) so attractive?
4. Most industrialized nations have had to do battle in the last few years with both recession and inflationary pressures. Yet shortsightedness both here and abroad causes each nation to feel that it is being asked to sacrifice too much. The popular ways of shifting the burdens include raising tariffs and cutting foreign aid. How can we fight this sort of "beggar-thy-neighbor," individualistic approach to our common dilemma?

3

Why Does
It Hurt
So Much?

We all feel inflation's fiscal impact. It does not take an economist to recognize that dollars buy less, or an accountant to realize that higher tax brackets take a proportionately larger bite out of our inflated incomes. But inflation also has a less obvious psychological impact. Consider this pair of facts: (1) People at all income levels except the top think that just 10 to 20 percent more income would bring more happiness.[1] (2) Even with our recent loss in buying power, the average American today enjoys a real disposable income (corrected for inflation and taxes) that is, as we have seen, 50 percent higher than in the 1950s. Our incomes have grown much faster than would have been needed to maintain a 1950 standard of living (see Figure 3.1). We have more cars, more color television sets, and more of all the outward signs of wealth than ever before. Since we believe that money increases happiness and since we do, in fact, have more money today than a few decades ago, we must be happier, right?

Wrong. We today are no more likely than those Americans of the 1950s to report feeling happy and satisfied with our lives. In 1957, for example, 35 percent reported themselves "very happy." By 1980, when our affluence had increased more than 50 percent, how many now declared themselves "very happy"? Only 33 percent! As Figure 3.2 shows, while Americans' affluence has risen dramatically, happiness has not. In fact, if we listen closely to the conversations around us, it appears that discontent has multiplied. "As people's spending outstrips their income, they feel and proclaim that they are underpaid, defeated by inflation and taxes, and incapable of affording their family's needs. Workers complain they cannot make ends meet on their inadequate salaries. Friends grouse to one another about rising costs and find bittersweet pleasure in itemizing [everything] they cannot afford. People living in lavish homes bemoan the cost of trivial items."[2] To paraphrase Sir Winston Churchill, it seems that never have so many people been so unthankful for so much. We have coined a word for this commiserating: *poortalk*.

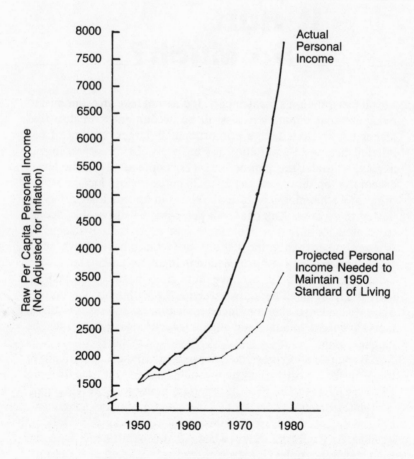

FIGURE 3.1. Has inflation defeated us? Here is a comparison of actual per capita personal income since 1950 with a projection adjusted for the annual rate of inflation. The gap between the lines reflects the growth of our prosperity over and above compensation for inflation.

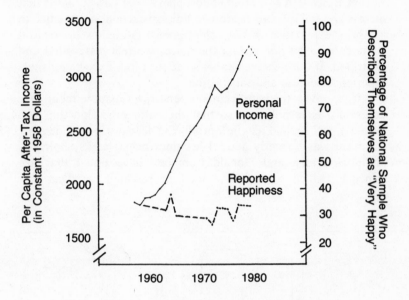

Figure 3.2. Does money buy happiness? Disposable income has doubled since the 1950s, but self-reported happiness has not increased.

When we affluent people succumb to poortalk, we reveal our insensitivity to the truly impoverished. It is the same type of insensitivity that is revealed when a slightly overweight person engages in self-pitying "fat talk," when an *A* student bemoans a mere *B* (thus demeaning the *B* that for many others is a significant achievement), or when a reasonably healthy person utters "sick talk," blithely forgetting the true agonies of those mortally ill. In each case, someone is taking for granted his or her "right" to be slender, academically superior, healthy, or without overdue bills.

Why all the poortalk? Why has the growth of our prosperity not been matched by an increase in our satisfaction with life? Several psychological principles combine to make us feel worse about our lot in life than is necessary. Becoming aware of these principles can help us understand the emotions that accompany our economic fluctuations.

Rising Expectations

The first principle is the *adaptation-level* phenomenon. Although research on this topic is relatively recent, the idea dates back to the ancient Epicurean and Stoic philosophers. The basic point is that success and failure, satisfaction and dissatisfaction, are relative to our prior experience. If our achievements fall below the neutral point defined by our prior experience, we feel dissatisfied and frustrated. If our achievements rise about those expectations, we experience success and satisfaction.

If, however, the improvements persist, we adapt to them. Our experience is recalibrated so that the color television that was formerly positive and pleasure-producing becomes merely neutral, and what was formerly neutral becomes negative. Psychologists Philip Brickman and Donald Campbell have noted that this principle, which is well grounded in research, predicts that

Figure 3.3. The adaptation-level phenomenon at work. The present looks pale in comparison to our memories of the "good old days."

Drawing by G. Kerlin; © 1978 The New Yorker Magazine, Inc.

humanity will never create a social paradise on earth. Once achieved, our utopia would soon be subject to recalibration so that we would again feel sometimes pleased, sometimes deprived, and sometimes neutral. Increased material goods, leisure time, or social prestige will give pleasure only initially. "Even as we contemplate our satisfaction with a given accomplishment, the satisfaction fades," note Brickman and Campbell, "to be replaced finally by a new indifference and a new level of striving."[3] The result is poortalk.

This is why, despite the increase in real income during the past several decades, the average American today reports no greater feeling of general happiness and satisfaction than he or she did twenty years ago. Moreover, cross-national surveys on rich and poor nations reveal few striking differences in self-reported happiness.[4] Egyptians are as happy as West Germans; Costa Ricans are as happy as Americans. "Poverty," said Plato, "consists not in the decrease of one's possessions but in the increase of one's greed." Assuming that inequality of wealth persists, there is a real sense in which we shall "have the poor among [us] always" (Mark 14:7). The poor remain poor partly because the criteria for poverty are continually redefined.

The principle of adaptation was plainly evident in the high suicide rate among people who lost their wealth during the depression. A temporary infusion of wealth can leave one feeling worse than if it had never come. For this reason, Christmas-basket charity may be counterproductive, making the recipient family more acutely aware of its poverty the other 364 days of the year while doing nothing to relieve the impoverished state.

A recent study of state lottery winners also illustrates the principle. Researchers at Northwestern University and the University of Massachusetts found that people felt good about winning the lottery. They typically said that it was one of the best things ever to happen to them. Yet their reported happiness did not increase. In fact, everyday activities like reading or eating breakfast became less pleasurable. It seemed that winning the lottery was such a high point that life's ordinary pleasures paled by comparison.[5] The phenomenon cuts both ways: Paraplegics, the blind, and other severely handicapped people generally adapt to their situations and eventually recover a normal or near-normal level of life satisfaction. Human beings have an enormous adaptive capacity. Victims of traumatic accidents would surely exchange places with those of us who are not paralyzed, and most of us would be delighted to win a state lottery. Yet, after a period of adjustment, none of these three groups departs appreciably from the others in moment-to-moment happiness.

The adaptation-level phenomenon implies that a period of slow growth or no growth in prosperity would have negative psychological effects, at least in the short run. The rapidly rising prosperity of recent decades has become embedded in people's consciousness and in their expectations for the future. We have gotten it into our heads that our affluence should continue to increase. In one University of Michigan survey, nearly half of those who reported feeling satisfied with their present standard of living said that the absence of further increases would be "disappointing" or even "disturbing."[6]

The adaptation-level principle, together with the fact that Americans most frequently mention their finances as their reason for being happy or unhappy, suggests that an end to economic growth would temporarily diminish happiness and satisfaction, even if the actual level of economic prosperity stayed the same. If we seek life satisfaction through material achievement, we will need a continually expanding level of affluence to maintain our old level of contentment.

Comparing Ourselves to Others

Whereas the adaptation-level phenomenon is rooted in changes in our own experience across time, the *relative-deprivation* principle is rooted in our comparison with other people.[7] The basic point is that success and failure, happiness and discontent, are also relative to what we observe others like ourselves experiencing. We evaluate our present experience not only in terms of some absolute internal standard of success or happiness, but also in relation to the rewards our peers receive. If our rewards surpass those received by comparable others, we are happy and contented; if our rewards fall below those received by our peers, we are indignant. A salary raise for a city's police officers will temporarily increase their morale, but it may deflate the morale of the fire fighters.

This principle is not new. As Karl Marx observed, "A house may be large or small; as long as the surrounding houses are equally small it satisfies all social demands for a dwelling. But let a palace arise beside the little house, and it shrinks from a little house to a hut."[8] Pieter Sorokin, a sociologist in the early 1900s, argued that "poverty or wealth of a man is measured, not by what he has at present but by . . . what others have."[9]

FIGURE 3.4. The relative-deprivation principle at work. Exposure to other people's wealth undermines our satisfaction with our own lot in life.

Drawing by Joseph Farris; © The New Yorker Magazine, Inc.

The relative-deprivation phenomenon has been supported by laboratory research and national surveys. In one survey of worker satisfaction, the workers in the deteriorated factory that had the worst pay and working conditions measured in the survey were not all that dissatisfied with their jobs. Conversely, workers in the best-paying factory were not as satisfied as expected. The researchers concluded that "it appeared that the constant exposure to the very high level [of affluence] which existed in this plant and community caused workers to shift the frame of reference against which they evaluated their [own] pay."[10] On a broader scale, Brickman and Campbell have suggested that Castro "may have raised the psychic well-being of the Cubans simply by getting rid of the rich tourists who came in numbers sufficient to constitute a very unfavorable comparison group."[11] If so, then Castro made a serious mistake by allowing exiles in the United States to return for family visits in 1979. The well-dressed, affluent exiles carrying color television sets as gifts may have generated enough relative deprivation to help spark the 1980 wave of refugees.

If human beings were perfectly objective, differences in the level of satisfaction would balance out. The lower half in any group would feel deprived, but the upper half would feel gratified. In reality *most* people in most groups feel deprived. At each income level Americans seem to want just about 25 percent more than they have, with only the extremely wealthy segment of society showing any sign of income satisfaction. The result? More poortalk.

Evaluating Ourselves

Two additional phenomena fuel the relative-deprivation experience. Recent psychological research has devoted considerable attention to a *self-serving bias* in our view of reality.[12] It is popularly believed that most of us suffer from the "I'm not OK—you're OK" problem of low self-esteem. As comedian Groucho Marx put it, "I'd never join any club that would accept a person like me." But the evidence now indicates that William Saroyan was much closer to the truth: "Every man is a good man in a bad world—as he himself knows."

Time and again, experiments have revealed that we take credit for our positive behaviors—"I donated money because I am a generous person"—while we blame our negative behaviors on external circumstances—"It wasn't my fault. I yelled at you because of what you did." Likewise, after working on a problem, people generally accept credit if successful (attributing the achievement to their ability and effort), yet attribute failure to such external factors as bad luck or the problem's inherent "impossibility." Students often exhibit the self-serving bias. Researchers have found that after receiving an examination grade, those who do well tend to accept personal credit by judging the exam as a valid measure of their competence. Those who do poorly are likely to criticize the exam as a poor indicator. Something or someone is always to blame. In experiments that require two people to cooperate in order to make money, most individuals blame their partner when the couple fails to cooperate. This illustrates a tendency evident in that first recorded excuse: "The woman you gave me . . ." (Genesis 3:12).

These findings are complemented by research that consistently reveals that, on a variety of dimensions, most people see themselves as better than average. For example, most see themselves as more ethical than their peers and as less prejudiced than others in their community. Most citizens view themselves as more concerned than their neighbors about assuring clean air and water and consuming less electricity. Such self-congratulation is not conducive to improved ethics or to further conservation efforts.

Recently, the College Entrance Examination Board invited the million high school seniors who took its aptitude test to indicate "how you feel compared with other people your age in certain areas of ability." Judging from their responses, it appears that America's high school seniors are not suffering from inferiority feelings. In "leadership ability," 70 percent rated themselves as above average, 2 percent as below average. Sixty percent viewed themselves as better than average in "athletic ability," but only 6 percent as below average. In "ability to get along with others," *zero* percent of the 829,000 students who responded rated themselves below average, 60 percent rated themselves in the top 10 percent, and 25 percent saw themselves among the top 1 percent![13]

These biased perceptions of our own abilities can lead to biased perceptions of our contributions to the success or failure of our groups. In a series of experiments, Barry Schlenker of the University of Florida had people work together on a task. He then gave them false information that suggested that their group had done either well or poorly. In every one of these studies the members of successful groups claimed more responsibility for their group's performance than did members of the groups that supposedly failed. Likewise, most presented themselves as contributing more than the others in their group when the group did well; few said they contributed less.[14] Such self-deception can lead people to expect greater-than-average rewards when their groups do well and less-than-average blame when they do poorly.

The human tendency to see oneself as more deserving than others is surely a source of much discontent. When a company or an institution awards merit salary raises, at least half of the employees will receive only an average raise or less. Since few see themselves as average or below, many will feel that an injustice has been done. The shortest line of all would be composed of those who feel they are overpaid. If, as one survey revealed, 94 percent of college faculty think themselves better than their average colleague, then when merit raises are announced and half receive an average raise or less, many will feel an injustice has been done them.

Note that a person's impression that he has been unjustly evaluated does not necessarily signify actual injustice. Even if God prescribed the salary increases according to his most perfect justice, many would still be upset unless their self-perceptions distributed themselves in conformity with the true distribution of employee excellence, which they surely would not. A fixed-percentage or fixed-increment salary increase does not resolve the problem. Many people may then feel that equal pay is, for them, inequitable, since they are more competent and committed than most of their colleagues.

The resentment that accompanies high inflation—even in times when wage increases keep pace with prices—partly reflects the self-serving bias. Economist George Katona has observed that people tend to perceive their wage increases as the reward for their talent and effort, and thus they see price increases as cheating them of gains that are rightfully theirs.[15]

The dissatisfactions bred by self-serving pride are compounded by another psychological phenomenon, *upward comparisons.* Laboratory experiments indicate that when people are given the opportunity to compare themselves with various other people, they generally choose to measure themselves against those whose performance or rewards have been superior rather than inferior to their own. Similarly, highly educated privates in World War II, whose chances of promotion were very good, exhibited more discontent with their prospects for promotion than did their less-educated peers who actually stood less chance of being promoted. The reason? Apparently the well-educated soldiers chose to compare themselves not with their fellow privates, but with their educated peers who had become officers.[16]

It seems that when climbing the ladder of social status, people look up, not down; their attention is focused on where they are going, not on the position from where they have come. This phenomenon of upward comparisons presents problems for social planning, since it partially negates the benefits of governmental policies designed to upgrade the educational and occupational levels of the lower-income segments of society. As a family or employee group increases in affluence and social status, it elevates the comparison standards by which it evaluates its own achievements. Paradoxically, this means that actual gains in income, possessions, or status may be offset by psychological losses stemming from the change in comparison group. Research suggests that "as blacks move up the economic and social scales, they become less satisfied . . . , more militant . . . , more alienated from the political system . . . , and more likely to take part in protest or riot activity . . . ."[17] Liberation movements, by raising their adherents' aspirations and expectations, may simultaneously stimulate increases in their actual achievements and in their perceived relative deprivation. Becoming a feminist is probably not initially going to alleviate a woman's frustration with her lot in life. In the short run, at least, she is as likely to feel more frustrated.

Psychologists have found no upper bounds for the rising aspirations embodied in this principle. The ladder seems infinite; so unless we renounce the climb, we will be forever comparing ourselves with others above us. We are like rats on a treadmill, requiring an ever-increasing level of income and social status just to feel neutral.

This sounds a bit pessimistic. Is there any cause for optimism? Taking a cynical viewpoint, we can draw some consolation from the fact that the adaptation-level principle works in both directions: If economic pressures force us to adopt a simpler lifestyle, we will eventually adapt and recover life's balance of happiness, discontent, and neutrality. But this approach is more traumatic than necessary, since the preceding principles can also be harnessed to speed up the recalibration and smooth the transition during a period of economic change. Moreover, this cynical approach robs us of the motivation to use each period of economic change as a challenging opportunity to reexamine our economic attitudes and behavior.

Questions for Further Consideration

1. Do you ever hear "poortalk"? What are some examples? How

might the same concerns have been expressed without self-pitying poortalk?

2. The average American does not report feeling happier now than in earlier, less prosperous times. How about you? Has your affluence increased? Has your happiness increased?

3. Are there items that you once thought were luxuries but that you now take for granted? How would you feel if you were suddenly deprived of those items?

4. Would your level of happiness and contentment with life change if your income dropped by 10 percent? How about 20 percent or 50 percent? In what ways would your psychological well-being be affected?

5. What do human beings *need?* What distinguishes a need from a want? Recall some of your recent purchases. Which were needs? Which were wants?

6. What emotions can money or the lack of it produce in you?

Responsible
Responses

Part 2

4

Where Do We Look for Guidelines?

We might well have concluded the first part of this book with the familiar closing words of Walter Cronkite, "And that's the way it is. . . ." For we have been reporters, not columnists. We have been describing our economic and psychological situation, not advocating responses to it. Thus, the Christian faith we share has been in the background until now. Chapters 1 and 2 have *not* been shaped by a "Christian economics," and Chapter 3 is *not* the product of a "Christian psychology."

Now we become columnists. Although the sciences describe our world, they cannot tell us how we ought to live. Should we, therefore, turn for guidance to the American way of life? It offers us a fairly coherent combination of habits, attitudes, and values to shape our economic life. By comparison with our personal opinions, it has the objectivity and legitimacy that derive from overwhelming public support. But God is God and we are creatures, and this is no less true when we get together in large groups.[1] Just as each of us individually is subject to God's word of judgment, so is the American way of life; it is as much in need of salvation and deliverance as are the private lives of those who make it up.

Therefore, as we turn now to the question of how we ought to respond to the present economic problems, we turn to our biblical faith for guidance. We believe that the biblical message applies to all aspects of our lives, including the economic; the Christian is not free to shape that life by secular principles. Stated in the language of the *Law*, we believe that our economic attitudes and behavior must be scrutinized by God's Word as revealed in the Bible. Stated in the language of the *gospel*, we believe that God's gracious covenant with us, culminated in Christ, brings wholeness and liberty to all of human life, including our economic attitudes and behavior. The bad news of judgment and the good news of grace go hand in hand; hence Jesus' announcement: "Repent; for the kingdom of Heaven is upon you" (Matthew 4:17).

Our proper response to the present economic situation is both inward and outward; it involves both our attitudes and our behavior. We want these responses to be responsible. For the Christian, responsibility is always evaluated in relation to God, the God who spoke in times past through prophets and apostles and, above all, through his Son, and who speaks to us today through the Bible. When we look at the responses with biblical spectacles, what are the responsible responses? What attitudes and behavior can withstand the scrutiny of the God revealed in the Bible?

Two principles of biblical faith serve as criteria for judging our personal and national responses: the *anti-materialism principle* and the *justice principle*.

Worship God Alone: The Anti-materialism Principle

It may seem strange to begin with a negative principle: *anti-materialism*. Is it not better to state *for* what you are rather than *against* what you are? Indeed, the principle in question here could easily be given an affirmative title, such as the contentment principle ("Godliness with contentment is great gain" [1 Timothy 6:6, KJV]) or the simplicity principle ("Consider the lilies . . ." [Matthew 6:28, KJV]). But two factors argue for stating the principle negatively. First, it reminds us of the biblical element we are usually most disposed to forget: the bad news, the divine judgment that calls humanity to repentence. Second, the Bible itself expresses the principle in negative language. More often than praising contentment or simplicity, it warns against the terrible danger of an inordinate desire for wealth.

Materialism is the idea that our life consists in the abundance of our possessions, that Jesus was wrong when he said, "Beware! Be on your guard against greed of every kind, for even when a man has more than enough, his wealth does not give him life" (Luke 12:15). Jesus and Paul list greed alongside the sins of sexual immorality, robbery, murder, and drunkenness (Mark 7:21-22; 1 Corinthians 6:9-10; Ephesians 5:5; Colossians 3:5), and Christian tradition has included it as one of the seven deadly sins.[2] Our own culture, by contrast, acknowledges only a single economic vice—stealing. "Greed" and "avarice" have been replaced with approving talk about "consumerism" and the "American dream." Although the

American dream once signified deliverance from grinding poverty, the dream has been constantly recalibrated upward so that the greed that Jesus and earlier Christians saw as sin has now become part of the dream.

The Bible's protests against trusting in riches are not unique. The traditional religious and philosophical wisdom of both East and West also counter greed with strong anti-materialism. Yet the biblical protests are distinctive. In opposition to those philosophies that view the material world as intrinsically evil and corrupt, biblical faith asserts that the physical creation is basically good, a good gift from the good God. Though all of God's gifts can be misused by human sinfulness, there is nothing wrong with material things as such. "For everything that God created is good, and nothing is to be rejected when it is taken with thanksgiving, since it is hallowed by God's own word and by prayer" (1 Timothy 4:4-5). Similarly, in the Old Testament we read, "Go to it then, eat your food and enjoy it, and drink your wine with a cheerful heart; for already God has accepted what you have done" (Ecclesiastes 9:7). Thus, the anti-materialism principle does not require us to despise the gifts of God; it, rather, insists that we do not live by bread alone, that our lives do not consist of material affluence, and that material things must not preempt our worship of God.

A second distinctive aspect of biblical anti-materialism can be seen by comparing these passages from Plato's *Republic* and the book of Proverbs. First, hear Socrates' comments about the dangers of wealth:

> Here then, is a discovery of new evils, I said, against which the guardians will have to watch, or they will creep into the city unobserved.
> What evils?
> Wealth, I said, and poverty; the one is the parent of luxury and indolence, and the other of meanness and viciousness, and both of discontent.[3]

Then listen to the sage's words in Proverbs 30:8-9—

> . . . Give me neither poverty nor wealth,
> provide me only with the food I need.
> If I have too much, I shall deny thee
> and say, 'Who is the LORD?'
> If I am reduced to poverty, I shall steal
> and blacken the name of my God.

In both passages it is clear that the fear of wealth is not based on any romantic illusions about poverty, nor does either passage make the point that the wealth of some means the poverty of others.

Rather, both focus on the danger of wealth to the wealthy.

But the passages also differ. For Plato wealth is dangerous because its by-products—luxury, indolence, and discontent—are harmful to both the individual and society. In Proverbs, by contrast, the emphasis is directly on our relation to God. Wealth tempts us to deny God. The primary question is not "How can I be happy?" but rather "How can I remain faithful to God?"

The same question lies at the heart of Deuteronomy 8. As the people are about to enter the Promised Land, Moses pleads with them, knowing how problematic is the prosperity they are about to inherit. He reminds them that they were first made hungry and then fed with manna to learn that "man cannot live on bread alone but lives by every word that comes from the mouth of the LORD" (v. 3). Now God is bringing them to a rich land: ". . . you will never live in poverty nor want for anything . . . . You will have plenty to eat and will bless the LORD your God for the rich land that he has given you" (vv. 9-10). It is just this blessing that bothers Moses:

> Take care not to forget the LORD your God and do not fail to keep his commandments . . . . When you have plenty to eat and live in fine houses of your own building, when your herds and flocks increase, and your silver and gold and all your possessions increase too, do not become proud and forget the LORD your God . . . . Nor must you say to yourselves, "My own strength and energy have gained me this wealth," but remember the LORD your God . . . (vv. 11-18).

This sensitivity to the inherent rivalry between our allegiance to wealth and to God lies at the heart of Jesus' astonishingly negative attitude toward riches. In Luke 12 his warning against greed and the teaching that "a person's true life is not made up of the things he owns, no matter how rich he may be" (v. 15, TEV) is followed by the story of the rich fool whose preoccupation with financial security led to a total neglect of his relation to God. When the same problem steps out of the parable into real life in the person of the rich young ruler, Jesus' words are even stronger: "How hard it is for the wealthy to enter the kingdom of God! It is easier for a camel to go through the eye of a needle than for a rich man to enter the kingdom of God" (Luke 18:24-25). Mark's version of this incident adds that the disciples were amazed that Jesus said this. But Jesus was only applying his teaching from the Sermon on the Mount that wealth (mammon) is a rival god. In an echo of Joshua's "choose here and now whom you will worship" (Joshua 24:15) Jesus insists upon a choice. "You cannot serve God and Money" (Matthew 6:24).

" I HAVE MY RELIGION... FRED HAS HIS "

Figure 4.1. Our worship at the altar of materialism has been enthusiastic but misguided.

This stark statement is sandwiched between two others that amplify it. First, we are warned against storing up treasure on earth instead of in heaven, since "where your treasure is, there will your heart be also" (v. 21). Since biblical religion is above all else a matter of the heart, anything that stands in the way of loving God with our whole heart is an idol. The jealous God of the Old Testament who will tolerate no rivalry from Baal here expresses his jealousy against money. Second, there is the warning against being anxious about material possessions and the invitation to consider instead the birds of the air and the lilies of the field (vv. 25-34). Here the question is one of trust. On what do we ultimately rely, God or money? This is the heart of the matter. Misplaced trust underlies misdirected desire. Only those who learn to trust and not be anxious about food, clothes, etc., will be able to avoid running after all these things, such as the heathen do, and to set their minds "on God's kingdom and his justice before everything else . . ." (v. 33).

On this topic, Paul is as blunt as Jesus. He twice equates greed with idolatry (Ephesians 5:5; Colossians 3:5). The Pastoral Epistles give special attention to greed, as when Timothy is warned:

> Those who want to be rich fall into temptations and snares and many foolish harmful desires which plunge men into ruin and perdition. The love of money is the root of all evil things, and there are some who in reaching for it have wandered from the faith and spiked themselves on many thorny griefs . . . . Instruct those who are rich in this world's goods not to be proud, and not to fix their hopes on so uncertain a thing as money, but upon God, who endows us richly with all things to enjoy. Tell them to do good and to grow rich in noble actions, to be ready to give away and to share, and so acquire a treasure which will form a good foundation for the future. Thus they will grasp the life which is life indeed (1 Timothy 6:9-10, 17-19).

It is especially important that a bishop be "no lover of money" and a deacon not given "to money-grubbing" (1 Timothy 3:3, 8; cf. Titus 1:7).

The Bible assumes that wealth's first danger is that it preempts our devotion to God, whereas Plato assumed wealth would interfere with self-fulfillment. Plato also assumed that vice and lack of fulfillment are due to ignorance, the remedy for which is good *advice*. The Bible, by contrast, *commands*. This difference between command and advice grows out of the earlier difference between placing God or ourselves in the center of the picture. Materialism, seen as a form of idolatry, is a violation of the first commandment. This is true whether by "first" we mean the first of the Ten Commandments—"You shall have no other gods before me" (Deuteronomy 5:7, RSV)—or the command that Jesus identifies as first and greatest—"Love the Lord your God with all your heart, with all your soul, with all your mind, and with all your strength" (Mark 12:30).

Loving Our Neighbors: The Justice Principle

If the anti-materialism principle is the economic dimension of the commandment to love the Lord our God with all our heart, the justice principle is the economic dimension of the commandment to love our neighbor as we love ourselves. In response to the question "Am I my brother's keeper?" the justice principle replies, "No, but you *are* his brother." It requires that I evaluate how my attitudes and behavior affect others, particularly the poor.

The biblical requirement that God's people care about the poor is grounded in the notion that God himself cares about them. For example, in Matthew 25:31-46 Jesus portrays the final judgment as a division of sheep from goats. Those who receive the Father's blessing and are welcomed into his kingdom are those to whom the Son of man can say, "For when I was hungry, you gave me food; when thirsty, you gave me drink; when I was a stranger you took me into your home, when naked you clothed me; when I was ill you came to my help, when in prison you visited me" (vv. 35-36). Those who fail to meet this test are cursed and sent to "the eternal fire that is ready for the devil and his angels" (v. 41).

Less familiar is another judgment scene from Psalm 82. God is presiding in the heavenly court to which he has called the gods for judgment. They are condemned to die as humans die for failing to uphold economic justice. They have not come to the aid of the weak, the orphan, the destitute, and the downtrodden, nor rescued the poor from the clutches of the wicked.

Both of these pictures convey the same central idea: God does not tolerate neglect of the poor. Both also contain a secondary idea. Matthew 25 indicates that God identifies with the poor so strongly as to count our behavior toward them as behavior toward him. "And the king will answer, . . . 'Anything you did [or did not do] for one of my brothers here, however humble, you did [or did not do] for me.' " (v. 40).[4] In Psalm 82, as in so many biblical passages, God asks not what the poor have done to deserve their plight, but of whose wicked power they are victims. These two ideas go together. God identifies with the poor because he sees how they have been victimized, and he sees how they have been victimized because he identifies with them.

The covenantal law of ancient Israel reveals the origin of God's concern for the poor. Israel is reminded that God delivered them from slavery in Eygpt not so they could take advantage of others, but to exhibit his justice in their life together. Israel's law constrained such activities as land ownership and use, moneylending, and conditions of employment in order to head off poverty before it got started and to alleviate whatever poverty might nevertheless occur. The laws of Jubilee, tithing, gleaning, the Sabbatical year, and the prohibition of usury all recognized that if the economic process were left to itself the people would quickly be divided into "haves" and "have-nots" and that this is unacceptable.

These laws expressed God's claim on his people's economic life on behalf of the poor.[5]

Against this background of covenantal law the prophets proclaim the judgment that overtakes first the Northern Kingdom and then the Southern Kingdom. Ancient Israel learned the hard way that God does not exempt his covenant people from his requirements of justice; he holds those who have received his law especially accountable for oppression or neglect of the poor, particularly the widows and orphans whose poverty is not their own fault. The prophet Amos, in particular, comes to mind in this context; but he is by no means alone. Sometimes the prophets protest taking advantage of the helpless. Thus Isaiah rebukes the leaders of the people:

> You have ravaged the vineyard,
>   and the spoils of the poor are in your houses.
> Is it nothing to you that you crush my people
>   and grind the faces of the poor?
> —Isaiah 3:14-15

And Jeremiah denounces the king:

> Shame on the man who builds his house by unjust means
>   and completes its roof-chambers by fraud,
>   making his countrymen work without payment,
>   giving them no wage for their labour! . . .
> Think of your father: he ate and drank,
> dealt justly and fairly; all went well with him.
> He dispensed justice to the lowly and poor;
> did not this show he knew me? says the LORD.
> But you have no eyes, no thought for anything but gain . . . .[6]
> —Jeremiah 22:13-17

On other occasions the prophets rebuke not overt oppression but indifference and neglect. In a surprising passage, Ezekiel says the sins of Jerusalem are even worse than those of Sodom. Rather than condemning Sodom for its infamous sexual excesses, Ezekiel proclaims: "This was the iniquity of your sister Sodom: she and her daughters had pride of wealth and food in plenty, . . . and yet she never helped the poor and wretched. They grew haughty and did deeds abominable in my sight, and I made away with them, as you have seen" (Ezekiel 16:49-50). Amos is no more tolerant:

> Shame on you who live at ease in Zion . . . !
> You who loll on beds inlaid with ivory
>   and sprawl over your couches,
> feasting on lambs from the flock
>   and fatted calves, . . .

> you who drink wine by the bowlful
> and lard yourselves with the richest of oils,
> but are not grieved at the ruin of Joseph.
>   —Amos 6:1, 4-6

The same dual response is found in the New Testament. James has a shrill word for those who have great possessions:

> Weep and wail over the miserable fate descending on you. Your riches have rotted . . . . You have piled up wealth in an age that is near its close. The wages you never paid to the men who mowed your fields are loud against you, and the outcry of the reapers has reached the ears of the Lord of Hosts. You have lived on earth in wanton luxury, fattening yourselves like cattle—and the day for slaughter has come. You have condemned the innocent and murdered him; he offers no resistance (James 5:1-6).[7]

Today's prophets are as sharp-tongued as Isaiah, Ezekiel, Amos, and James. They argue that "those of us who live comfortably in the rich world cannot avoid the knowledge that our affluence is based on the misery of the desperately poor,"[8] that the spoils of the poor are indeed in our houses.*

But perhaps we are being unfair to affluent Christians. Perhaps we have left something out. Does God not promise economic prosperity to the upright? And can we not, therefore, view our prosperity as a sign of his approval?

The answer to the first question is "Yes, but . . . ." The answer to the second question is simply no. There surely are passages where God promises material blessings to those who are faithful. (See, for example, Deuteronomy 6–8; 28; Leviticus 26; Psalms 72; 112.) The book of Proverbs is especially filled with the "peace and prosperity in righteousness" theme. *But,* this is primarily an Old Testament theme. The New Testament casts a new light on this theme with reminders that following Christ means taking up the cross. The disciples of Jesus are not promised anything better in this life than their Master received for his obedience.

There is a second qualification to the yes that answers the question, "Does God not promise to prosper the righteous?" Righteousness is defined as faithfulness to the covenant, and the covenant law prominently features various expressions of the

---

*However, some economists would dispute the notion that poor nations and poor persons are poor precisely because the rich are rich. Instead, they argue that most of the poor are poor primarily because they possess few of the resources that bring good market prices. This implies that the poor can best be helped out of poverty *not* by outright income grants nor by attempts to regulate prices, but rather by efforts to improve their resource base (e.g., land reform, education and assistance in development of new technologies) and their political power.

anti-materialism and justice principles. The promise of blessing does not stand in conflict with the stern requirements of these two principles; rather, they are essential conditions for the reward of prosperity. Thus, the promise gives new prominence to the principles. And since the New Testament makes it clear that God's concern is not merely national but global, the justice principle takes on an even more dramatic meaning. The poor and oppressed whom we must not neglect no longer live simply "across the tracks" but also across the sea.

What, then, about the second question: Is our prosperity a sign of God's approval? No, not necessarily. On this answer, the Old and New Testaments agree. As Ron Sider puts it, "the Bible does teach that God rewards obedience with prosperity. But it denies the converse. It is a heresy, particularly common in the West, to think that wealth and prosperity are always a sure sign of righteousness. They may be the result of sin and oppression as in the case of Israel."[9] Remember that when the prophets warned of God's judgment upon Israel's wealthy and powerful, the prophets pointed to their wealth as evidence of their *disobedience* rather than God's favor.

The "heresy" involved in assuming wealth to be a sign of b.essing rests on illogical thinking. Even if God prospers those who are faithful, it does not logically follow that "If I am prosperous, I must have been faithful." Al Capone was prosperous, but for reasons other than his faithfulness to God.

For all of this my wealth may still be God's blessing on my obedience. But even if we are fully persuaded that we are not the beneficiaries of unjust world economic systems or of unethical business practices, we face the gentler though perhaps even more devastating words of 1 John 3:17-18—"But if a man has enough to live on, and yet when he sees his brother in need shuts up his heart against him, how can it be said that the divine love dwells in him? My children, love must not be a matter of words or talk; it must be genuine, and show itself in action."

This latter theme is especially prominent in Jesus' teaching. Both in the Matthew 25 division of sheep and goats and in the parable of the rich man and Lazarus (Luke 16:19-31), people are held responsible for failing to help feed the hungry—not because they were in some direct way responsible for the plight of the poor, but simply because they were able to help and did not. Similarly, Jesus advised both the rich young ruler and the disciples to give to the poor (Luke 18:22; 12:33).[10]

All this indicates why seeking after wealth is a hindrance to giving God's kingdom highest priority. For God's kingdom not only requires that God alone be God in our lives, but also that we see the poor as God sees them—as our brothers and sisters in God's family—and, thus, that we neither oppress nor neglect them. It also becomes clearer why the new "covenant-kingdom" that Jesus brings can be described as good news to the poor (Luke 4:18; 7:23). Being in God's kingdom not only requires the "haves" to share generously with the "have-nots," but it also frees the wealthy for "koinonia"—the fellowship of total sharing[11]—by teaching that our lives consist not in the abundance of our possessions but in the love of God and neighbor.

Questions for Further Consideration

1. Who are materialists? Those who have material abundance? Or those who so desire material prosperity that they step on people in their clamor to get more of it?
2. What biblical themes underlie the idea that each nation's way of life stands under God's judgment and needs his salvation? What are the practical implications of such a view?
3. Why are the commandments to love God and neighbor so seldom given an economic interpretation in the preaching and teaching of the church?
4. Do we really treat stealing as more serious than greed? If so, why?
5. In what different ways is prosperity spiritually dangerous?
6. Why does the Bible treat neglect of the poor on a par with actively oppressing them?
7. What barriers have to be overcome if we are to hear the prophets' message addressed *to us?*

5

Changing Our Attitudes

Why Change?

The biblical guidelines described in the previous chapter help motivate and direct changes in our attitudes and behavior. These guidelines serve both as a mirror that allows us to see ourselves as we really are (James 1:23-25) and as a light that illuminates the path we ought to be taking (Psalm 119:105). No matter which analogy we choose, most of us realize that our thoughts and actions are not in obedience with God's commands; we are not living up to the standards he has set for us.

We need only look around us to see the physical and psychological consequences of our generation's economic attitudes. For decades America's prosperity has been the envy of much of the world; yet the way in which we have achieved our "economic blessings" has taken a toll on the quality of our environment, on the world's nonrenewable resources, on our relationships with other countries, and on our own personal values and family life. The dramatic growth in our standard of living has brought with it a new creed: "More, further, quicker, richer."[1]

We thought that living by this new creed would bring increased happiness and personal satisfaction with life. Instead, the rising expectations and unwise comparisons discussed in chapter 3 have combined to multiply economic discontent. In an anonymous editorial in the *New York Times*,[2] a thirty-year-old editor informed us that, although his yearly income was $30,000, he was in such severe financial distress that he had to draw upon his meager savings just to pay the bills for his family's "no-frills lifestyle." Because of rising "fixed" monthly expenses—including $30 for newspapers, $30 for dry cleaning, $200 for transportation (not including car payments), and $200 for past department store and credit card purchases—he could no longer afford to buy lamb chops or take exciting vacations. His lifestyle would be the envy of billions of people around the world; yet he feels frustrated and cheated: "I have earned the right to have more for myself and my family, to have what I earn get us more of what this city and country have to offer." Not only has poortalk's myopia blinded him to the needs of others, but it has also soured his enjoyment of the things that he has.[3]

We also thought that living by the new creed of "more, further, quicker, richer" would solve society's ills. Many have argued that rapid economic growth is the only way to alleviate poverty, that the "trickle-down effect" would eventually raise the standard of living for the poor in both America and the Third World countries.[4] While it is true that America's poor are generally well-off by global standards, decades of economic growth have not been a cure-all. Our worship at the altar of economic growth has been enthusiastic but misguided. Economic growth has many benefits, but of itself it produces neither economic justice nor happiness.

Perhaps it is time to change our economic attitudes. Perhaps it is time to bring them into conformity with the biblical anti-materialism and justice principles, placing not wealth but God's will at the center of our lives. For Christians, obedience to God's commands is sufficient motivation for such a change. But fitting our lives into God's plan also benefits us. By changing our attitudes, we can maximize our personal happiness and contentment with life. Since our rising expectations and unwise comparisons make us feel worse than necessary about our economic condition, changing our attitudes and expectations can make us *feel* better about ourselves and more contented with our lifestyles, regardless of our actual income.

Also, changing our economic attitudes can help us do our part to slow the reckless consumption of the earth's resources and the buildup of hazardous wastes. If we treat God's creation with respect and dignity, future generations may also be able to experience its beauty and life-sustaining abundance.[5]

What Changes Should We Make?

The "more, further, quicker, richer" attitude produced by decades of rapidly rising prosperity and amplified by our sins of pride and greed is deeply embedded in our consciousness and expectations, so deeply that a radical transformation is needed. We need a whole

new way of thinking and feeling; we need a "new mind." Paul did
not share our economic problems, but he was aware of the need for
radical transformations: "Adapt yourselves no longer to the pattern
of this present world, but let your minds be remade and your whole
nature thus transformed. Then you will be able to discern the will of
God, and to know what is good, acceptable, and perfect" (Romans
12:2).

But how are we to change such deeply embedded attitudes?
Psychological research has demonstrated that attitudes, especially
important ones, are surprisingly resistant to change, even in the face
of contrary evidence. That resistance can be understood in
theological terms. Some of our economic attitudes are rooted in the
pride and greed of our sinful nature, and by ourselves we are
powerless to overcome the sin that separates us from God. Thus, we
cannot merely decide to change our attitudes and overnight expect
to see a radical transformation. But with the help of the Spirit, who
daily gives us power to overcome evil and live God's will, we can
take the first steps down the long road to a new way of thinking.

What are some of those steps? The first is to redefine what it
means to be happy. In national surveys when people are asked to
rate their present happiness or satisfaction with life, they most often
mention personal economic considerations as the reason for recent
changes in their happiness or discontent.[6] Money in the pocket
means happiness, while overdue bills mean unhappiness. This
"money equals happiness" attitude is widely held and is reinforced
by the media. Advertisements for everything from luxury cars to
Caribbean vacations serve to whet our consumer appetites, and
credit card companies assure us that the doors to the "good life" will
open at the touch of "plastic money."

But does money really bring happiness? If we analyze our
present life satisfaction, pinpointing recent changes in wealth or
possessions, what will we find? (Take another look at Figure 3.2 on
page 35.) Most of us will discover that past fluctuations in income or
material possessions have had only a transient impact on our
happiness. "If you love money, you will never be satisfied; if you
long to be rich, you will never get all you want. It is useless"
(Ecclesiastes 5:10, TEV). It is fitting that the Declaration of
Independence specifies only the *pursuit* of happiness as an
inalienable right, since our elation over a raise in pay or an
unexpected inheritance always fades into neutrality, only to be
replaced by a new craving for an even higher level of income and
possessions.[7] We are like the child who races after soap bubbles in

the wind, only to see each one vanish just as it is grasped.

This is the adaptation-level phenomenon at work, employed in the service of our sinful greed. But just becoming aware of this principle can help us gain mastery over it. Recognizing that our economic "wants" and "needs" are relative to our past experience can help diminish the pain that occurs when those "wants" cannot be afforded. Recognizing our past captivity to our material appetites can help us escape from that slavery now. If we know that our getting that newer home, taking that nicer vacation, owning that

"Are you satisfied now that you've reached the top, J.P., or will you strive to reach the tippy-top?"

FIGURE 5.1. Our elation over recent achievements soon fades into neutrality, to be replaced by a new level of striving.

Drawing by H. Martin; © 1979 The New Yorker Magazine, Inc.,

larger stereo system will ultimately leave us no happier than we are now, we may be freed for greater enjoyment of the pleasures we now have.

As we seek to redefine our happiness not in terms of the growth of our income or possessions, nor in terms of some arbitrary level of material wealth, we would do well to consider what Jesus said about happiness in his Sermon on the Mount:[8] How happy are those who are humble, who are merciful, who are pure in heart, who work for peace. Rather than defining happiness as something reserved for the rich and powerful, Jesus proclaims that happiness belongs in a special way to those who are poor, who mourn, and who suffer for the gospel. This is not to say that grief, poverty, and pain are in themselves "blessed"; nowhere does the Bible teach a "Kick me again, God" masochism. The poor and the mourning are blessed precisely because the obstacles coming between them and God have been removed; the kingdom is theirs! The rich and powerful are tempted to depend on their own resources, while the poor and suffering acknowledge their dependence on God and are open to his gracious intervention.

> "Happy are those whose
> greatest desire is to do
> what God requires;
> God will satisfy them fully!"
> —Matthew 5:6, TEV

Not only can we change our attitudes about happiness, but we can also redefine what we mean by "success." The American dream defines success in economic terms. The successful businessperson has a six-figure income. The successful movie actor has a million-dollar contract. The successful author lands huge advances. The manner in which income or possessions are acquired is almost irrelevant: the inventor of the "pet rock" contributed little to human well-being; yet the money he earned labels him as a "success."

Equating success with wealth is not without justification. Many of the wealthy are reaping the rewards of their competence and hard work. But there have always been equally dedicated individuals whose hard work has not produced economic rewards. As the Preacher of Ecclesiastes states: ". . . Wise men do not always earn a living, intelligent men do not always get rich, and capable men do not always rise to high positions . . ." (Ecclesiastes 9:11, TEV). What makes this a problem is the degree to which our individual feelings of self-worth are intertwined with our notion of success.

Economic success somehow gives value and dignity to an otherwise ordinary life. To be rich is to be "somebody"; the wealthy person has "made it" in a way that a poor man never could. The Preacher goes on to tell a story about a poor man who was so clever he could have saved his town from destruction, but no one listened to him because "no one thinks of a poor man as wise, or pays any attention to what he says" (Ecclesiastes 9:16, TEV).

Such thinking illustrates what social psychologists now call "the just world hypothesis."[9] Most people seem to assume that this is a just world, that people deserve what they get. From childhood we learn that rewards come to those who are good and punishments to those who are bad. From this it is but a short leap to assuming (as people in social-psychological experiments often do) that those who are rewarded *must* be good and those who are punished also *must* have deserved their fate. Job's three friends illustrated this "just world" thinking when they argued that his suffering was surely brought on by his own sin. While it is true that effort and wisdom are often rewarded, the just world assumption can also lead people to justify economic injustice and to assume mistakenly that the wealthy *must* merit their wealth. Thus, being wealthy gives the person power to influence the lives of others, to make his or her opinions known, to command effortlessly the respect of the community in a way that "lesser" individuals can only envy.

But success is as elusive as happiness. Proverbs 23:4-5 (TEV) cautions: "Be wise enough not to wear yourself out trying to get rich. Your money can be gone in a flash, as if it had grown wings and flown away like an eagle."

Tom Minnery tells a story about a sports hero who learned this lesson. After achieving superstardom with the Buffalo Bills football team, O. J. Simpson was traded to the San Francisco 49ers and became a second-string player.

> One day he told a teammate: "Fame is a vapor, popularity an accident, and money takes wings."
> The friend asked where he'd heard that. O. J. replied: "I was watching a late hockey game on TV one night, and all of a sudden a guy just said it. Brought me right out of my chair. I never forgot it."[10]

A sudden increase in wealth or the status that wealth brings makes us feel successful, but the feeling gradually disappears if our level of income or status does not continue to increase. This is the adaptation-level principle at work again, and its power is evident even in the way we talk about success. For example, the most impressive type of success is the "rags-to-riches" phenomenon, the

Hi and Lois   ®   **By Mort Walker & Dik Browne**

FIGURE 5.2. Getting off the treadmill is not easy.

rapid (and often unexpected) rise from poverty to wealth. But what happens if the newly rich individual merely maintains that level of wealth? Is success, once earned, a permanent attribute? The answer seems to be negative. To maintain the feeling of success, the newly rich individual must strive for more riches. In the absence of new achievements, the perception of success fades into neutrality. All of us are on a "success treadmill"; we need a constantly increasing level of wealth and status to maintain our feeling of success. The only way to break the cycle, to insulate ourselves from fluctuations in our economic condition, is to get off the treadmill, to stop "chasing the wind" (Ecclesiastes 4:4)

Redefining success means placing value on our hard work and achievements, regardless of whether we receive economic rewards. If we can view our labors as intrinsically of value to ourselves, or as contributing to the welfare of others, we may be freed from the need to evaluate our success or lack of it in economic terms. For example, child care workers and nursery school teachers often receive little more than the minimum wage. If they were to evaluate the importance of their job in terms of their salaries, they would conclude that the work they are doing has little value. However, if they were to move away from an economic definition of importance to one that reflects the challenging opportunities to shape young minds, these individuals might experience the satisfaction they deserve. This is not meant to commend a blind tolerance of economic injustice. Rather, we should distinguish carefully between those things that are within our power to change and those that are not. If the source of the perceived injustice is subject to our control, then we should struggle mightily to correct the problem. But if it lies outside our power, we should accept the situation with equanimity.

Finally, redefining success means placing value on our present economic condition, even if it is not improving. Here a careful choice of comparison groups can help us. We can resist the tendency to measure ourselves against those who are higher on the ladder of success or who are moving up more rapidly than we are. Instead, we can choose to compare ourselves with those who are less fortunate.

As Abraham Maslow noted: "(. . . . All you have to do is to go to a hospital and hear all the simple blessings that people never before realized *were* blessings—being able to urinate, to sleep on your side, to be able to swallow, to scratch an itch, etc.) Could *exercises* in deprivation educate us faster about all our blessings?"[11] A research team led by Marshall Dermer put University of Wisconsin-Milwaukee women through imaginative exercises in deprivation. After viewing grim depictions of how bad life was in Milwaukee in 1900, or after imagining and writing about various personal tragedies, such as being burned and disfigured, the women expressed increased satisfaction with the quality of their own lives.[12]

Earlier generations were taught to perform such comparisons as a way of "counting one's blessings." Today we can gain the same benefit by means of selective exposure to comparison groups. Our fragile feelings of success are likely to vanish in situations where we are surrounded by other people's luxury and wealth. Since such settings emphasize the economic connotations of success, we can best nurture a different set of attitudes if we avoid those situations. On the other hand, we can go out of our way to confront true poverty, to drown our relative deprivations in the sea of real deprivation that exists for so many people.

Discovering how relatively small our problems are can make us more sensitive to genuine deprivation. It can give us an appreciation of the extent to which some people's unmet needs—clean water, adequate nutrition, medical care—are things we take for granted. Realizing this will not only sensitize us to the suffering of the truly impoverished, but it will also help us develop an attitude of gratitude for what we have. And if we are genuinely grateful, we will be empowered to use our wealth individually and collectively to meet the needs of others.

But we cannot just snap our fingers and expect to see radical changes in our attitudes. The process of "remaking our minds" is long and challenging. That is why we need to make a point of finding others who have similar attitudes and values. Seeing them engaged in the same struggle can help reinforce our own efforts, and their successes can serve as models for the changes we have yet to make. The mutual support in a community of concerned Christians can help all of us complete the transformation by not only changing the way we think, but also by changing the way we live.

Questions for Further Consideration

1. Is there anything wrong with our economic attitudes? Do we really need to change?
2. When you were growing up, was there ever a drastic change in your family's income? How did your family respond?
3. Will it really do any good to redefine intellectually the criteria for happiness and success?
4. Do people deserve what they get? Are the rich wealthy because they are smart and work hard? Are the poor lazier and more irresponsible?
5. How do you feel about your present income? Is it more or less than you deserve?
6. Would exercises in deprivation help change your attitudes? If so, would the attitude change be permanent, or would you have to keep repeating the exercise?
7. Can simpler living be imposed on people, or must it be voluntary? How would you feel if your employer introduced a "simpler living" pay scale that included 10 percent pay cuts for everyone, with the money going to a worthy cause? Would this approach work?

6

Changing Our Behavior

Changed behavior is as important as changed attitudes for a responsible response to the economic situation. The biblical emphasis on the heart makes it impossible for us to ignore attitudes, but we must be careful not to misinterpret this emphasis. The Bible refuses to separate the inner and outer dimensions of life and give primacy to the inner. Thus, we draw conclusions that Scripture does not support when we say that our economic behavior is not really important as long as we have the right attitude toward wealth. For all its emphasis on the heart, the Bible keeps calling us to action. James reminds us that faith without works is dead (James 2:17; cf. 1 John 3:18). Far from disagreeing, Paul says he is called "to lead to faith and obedience" those who have heard the call and belong to Jesus (Romans 1:5-6), and he fills his epistles with guidance as to what that obedience entails. And Jesus tells his disciples, " 'You are my friends, if you do what I command you' " (John 15:14). He even incorporates this idea into the Great Commission. He sends his disciples forth not to make mere converts, but disciples like themselves. This Great Commission also includes the charge to "teach them to observe all that I have commanded you" (Matthew 28:19).

There is a psychological as well as a theological reason why obedience and faith go together: Our behavior shapes our attitudes as much as our attitudes shape our behavior. When we act, we amplify the idea lying behind what we have done. This is one of the most interesting and extensively documented discoveries of recent social-psychological research, and it has direct implications for the Christian life. Behavior contrary to biblical principles will contaminate the heart by generating attitudes consistent with that behavior. In experiments, people who harm someone—by delivering electric shocks, for example—tend to express disdain for their victim. Evil acts shape the self. But, happily, the opposite is equally true. Doing the deeds of love for God and neighbor can amplify loving attitudes.[1] Jesus knew this principle and applied it to our economic life when he said, "For where your treasure is, there will your heart be also" (Matthew 6:21). We often read this as if Jesus had said that our treasure would be where our heart is. While it may be true that we can check up on our attitudes by taking a hard look at our budgetary behavior, Jesus is suggesting that we can also change our heart's attachments by redirecting our investments from financial security to the work of his kingdom.

If attitudes and behavior are the inner and outer dimensions of life, we can also distinguish the inward-directed from the outward-directed aspects of behavior itself. Behavioral changes can be oriented toward changing ourselves or toward working with others to change the world in which we live. Remembering that Jesus spoke rather harshly of those who worry about the faults of others before tending to their own (Matthew 7:3-5), we would do well to look first at changing our own behavior.

Action Toward Changing Ourselves

Perhaps the place to begin in changing ourselves is with learning activities. Thanks to the media we have a steady supply of data about the state of the American economy; but many Christians have a surprisingly shallow grasp of biblical teaching about wealth and poverty, and only a vague image of those large portions of the world's population that do not share the luxury of our middle-class economic anxieties. Many ministers are reluctant to preach about money and stewardship, perhaps from the honorable but misguided motive of not wishing to seem preoccupied with money. All of us are more comfortable thinking as little as possible about the world's really poor people, a point nicely illustrated by the following incident. During the Sahel famine of the early seventies a national news magazine had a cover picture of a malnourished African child with a bloated belly signifying kwashiorkor. Out of curiosity a receptionist saw to it that the waiting room copy was regularly placed cover up on the table. Probably no one consciously turned the magazine over, saying, "I do not wish to see this picture." But whenever the receptionist returned to check, she found it turned over and, thus, out of sight. An important feature of our whole society is revealed in this little incident.

Learning Activities

We need to take steps, then, to increase both our biblical knowledge and our global knowledge. Right reading is itself a responsible response to the present economic crisis. With regard to our biblical knowledge, a good place to start is with the Bible itself. One young man was told that God says we should care about the poor. To find out if this was so, he read the Bible from cover to cover; each time he came to some teaching about wealth or poverty, he wrote it down on a slip of paper. His whole outlook on life was changed by his discovering for himself the anti-materialism and justice principles.

The same is true on the global front. There is a "wealth" of books about poverty in the United States and especially in the Third World, where the depth and breadth of poverty are greatest. Anyone who wants to learn about the plight of the poor and how they are affected by our consumption patterns, corporate investment practices, and governmental policies will be overwhelmed with a large and growing literature.

For starters, we recommend two highly readable books written from a Christian perspective. Arthur Simon's *Bread for the World* gives a picture of poverty and hunger both in the United States and abroad. He shows in detail how the trade, aid, investment, military, and environmental policies of the "haves" affect the daily lives of the "have-nots." Ronald Sider's *Rich Christians in an Age of Hunger* focuses on the concept of structural evil to emphasize that the political and economic practices that perpetuate poverty are, for the most part, legal and taken for granted. But his careful study of biblical teaching on wealth and poverty shows that the God of the Exodus, the Exile, and the incarnation is opposed to those who practice "mischief under cover of law" (Psalm 94:20). Both books make suggestions about Christian responses to the plight of the poor and give guidance for further reading.

We also recommend several other books on international poverty written by economists. *The Rich Nations and the Poor Nations* by Barbara Ward, *The Widening Gap: Development in the 1970s* edited by Barbara Ward and others, *The Challenge of World Poverty* and *Asian Drama: An Inquiry into the Poverty of Nations* by Gunnar Myrdal, and *The Nature of Mass Poverty* by John K. Galbraith all contain helpful insights.

We suggest the following threefold rationale to motivate and give direction to this reading: (1) Knowing about the poor is a prerequisite to caring about them and helping them. The biblical justice principle calls upon us to learn about the Lazaruses outside our door. (2) The biblical anti-materialism principle calls upon us to be less attached to our wealth and less anxious about it. Since our tendency to compare ourselves with those who are an economic step ahead breeds dissatisfaction, reversing this habit by reading about those *less* fortunate can help us begin to replace wealth addiction with compassion and gratitude. (3) Learning about the poor is not the kind of learning that is done for its own sake, as if it were enough to know about poverty and be against it. Rather, it is intended to lead to other kinds of activity and to give meaning and purpose to those actions.

Learning about poverty is one thing. Getting to know the poor is another. Statistical and analytical accounts of poverty and its causes need to be joined with a more concrete, personal kind of learning. Senator Ernest F. Hollings of South Carolina tells what this kind of learning meant to him:

> I was a victim of hunger myopia. I didn't really see hunger until I visited some families in a Charleston, South Carolina slum. Before we had gone a block, I was miserable. I began to understand that hunger is real, that it exists in hundreds of humans in my own home city. I saw what all America needs to see. The hungry are not able-bodied men, sitting around drunk and lazy on welfare. They are children. They are abandoned women, or the crippled, or the aged.[2]

Bridging the barrier of economic segregation and becoming acquainted with the poor near our own homes might do more to help us understand what Jesus and the prophets were talking about than anything else we could do.

Firsthand knowledge of Third World poverty is also a very real possibility for many. For example, those who can afford a Caribbean vacation could also afford to spend some time getting acquainted with the islands' poor. To see the large, fertile plain in Jamaica where sugar is grown for export and then to talk with the desperately poor cane cutters, to see the miles upon miles of urban shantytowns and then to talk with some of the residents who have no work at all—this is to have on a global scale the kind of experience Senator Hollings talks about on a national scale.

We can almost have this kind of experience without stepping outside our house. After reading *Child of the Dark* (Carolina M. De Jesus), the journal of a Brazilian ghetto mother, we come away almost knowing what it is like to have our daughter say, "Mama, sell me to Dona Julita, because she has delicious food" (p. 42). We can meet other anguished parents of those same Brazilian shantytowns with Walter Stanley Mooneyham of World Vision by reading his *What Do You Say to a Hungry World?* We can meet Pitung, resident of a virtually identical shantytown halfway around the world in Indonesia, and nearby in the Philippines we can meet José and learn why he is angry about the plight of landless peasants in an economy oriented to export for profit. Closer to home we can meet Alberto, a cane cutter in the Dominican Republic who works harder than we have ever thought of working, but who lives in desperate poverty while the American company he works for makes handsome profits from his labor.[3]

In summary, we suggest three kinds of learning activities as an initial response to our present economic situation: (1) careful study of biblical teaching about wealth and poverty; (2) reading about poverty, its scope, its causes, and its consequences; (3) getting personally acquainted with the poor, in person and through books and other media.

Since an important function of these learning activities is to reshape our attitudes about both the poor and our possessions, they should not themselves be turned into a new kind of possession. The task is not to stockpile more and more knowledge in ever larger intellectual barns. If we do this, our knowledge is likely to sour into sullenness, despair, and the guilt that breeds resentment rather than repentance. In addition, the attitude changes that begin to take root will be choked by more deeply rooted patterns of behavior. Given the already mentioned priority of behavior over attitudes, we need to find a new avenue of behavioral change that will put our knowledge to work and nourish the emerging attitudes it is shaping. Given the decision to deal with our own lives first, we are brought to a question given increasing attention among Christians today: Should we deliberately alter our lifestyles in the direction of living more simply?

Lifestyle Changes

Simpler living is a challenge directed toward our behavior as consumers. It means, quite simply, consuming less. It means rediscovering the distinction between what we need and what we want; it means taking positive steps to repudiate the philosophy underlying the ad for a certain fabric softener that Mrs. America, the perfect homemaker, finds to be a "necessary luxury." It means trying to act out the distinction between needs and wants in the light of the biblical anti-materialism and justice principles. It means praying to be pruned. (Try reading John 15:1-2 in this light.)

Simplifying our lifestyles is something similar to cleaning a garage or basement. That is a task that is never completed once and for all. In most of our lives it is a job we must come back to again and again, though ideally it is more nearly the constant activity of not letting things get out of control. This cleaning involves both getting rid of the junk that does not belong there and putting the things that do belong in their proper places. When this is done, there is room in the cleaned-out space for the things and activities it was intended to house. Simpler living is a way of uncluttering our lives so as to make room for God and neighbor, including our own families.

Another helpful image is that of stepping off the treadmill. The psychology of poortalk has shown us that we are consumed by the consumer ethic, that the attempt to fill the emptiness in our lives with possessions is self-defeating. Since each new level of affluence becomes the basis for desiring still more and comparing ourselves with those still a notch higher, we are like rats on a treadmill, exerting great quantities of energy but getting nowhere. As William Stringfellow has perceptively put it, the poverty that comes to expression in poortalk is a new poverty whose earmarks are not malnutrition or inadequate housing, but the spiritual and psychological exhaustion that come from preoccupation with keeping up and getting ahead.[4]

A pastor in our town recently gave expression to ideas like this in his prayer. He asked God to help us to be less attached to our possessions so that we might "travel lightly" through the world in the service of God's kingdom. One member of the congregation was especially offended by this reference. After referring to the depression, she said that having money in the bank was the most satisfying experience of her life. One does not have to deny that there was genuine suffering during the depression to hear a real tragedy in those words on the lips of a Christian. They express a sad commentary on both her understanding of her faith and on the Christian teaching to which she had been exposed for years.

Before we pray too quickly, "Lord, I thank thee that I am not like that woman," let us hear the words of our Lord. Let those who have never taken greater pleasure in their material blessings than in their spiritual ones cast the first stones. If changing our behavior as consumers is to be serious and sustained, and if it is to be something more than a "simpler-than-thou" ego trip, we will all need help. One of our most basic needs will be a clear understanding of just what we are up to. Since we do not want to deny the goodness of creation, we cannot embrace an asceticism that treats material

FIGURE 6.1. "Simpler than thou."

objects as intrinsically evil. And if that is not our rationale, what will be?

We suggest the following fourfold rationale:

1. *Obedient celebration.* God has endowed us richly with all things to enjoy, but at the same time warned us about the danger of wealth. Simpler living for affluent Christians means trying to take both of these facts seriously. It involves the celebrative enjoyment of the good things God has given us without letting the gifts replace the giver in our hearts. At the same time it means celebrating *all* the gifts God has given us, not just the material gifts our culture has tended to make preeminent. The anti-materialism principle (but not hostility to possessions as such) is at work here.

2. *Solidarity and sharing with the poor.* "The rich must live more simply so that the poor may simply live." There are two dimensions to this. In choosing to live more nearly as the poor are compelled to live, we make a gesture of solidarity with those who have no choice about their lifestyle. This can become more than an empty gesture, for at the same time we can free more of our financial resources to share with those whose needs are truly desperate. In times of economic crisis church giving tends to suffer, especially for benevolences. As the needs of the truly poor intensify, available help diminishes. Simpler living is a way of sharing more, even in times when inflation and taxes tempt us to think only of ourselves. The justice principle is at work here.

3. *Authentic witness.* By doing what our Lord has taught, we give witness in the church and in the world that he is indeed our Lord. This gives integrity both to evangelistic proclamation and to any political action to which we may be led. In terms of evangelism, "it is impossible with integrity to proclaim Christ's salvation if he has evidently not saved us from greed, or his lordship if we are not good stewards of our possessions, or his love if we close our hearts against the needy."[5] In terms of politics, our advocacy of a society

FIGURE 6.2. "We decided we'd denied ourselves color long enough—but that no one who's sensitive to the plight of the world's poor should go beyond a 21-inch set."

Drawing by Albert A. Bell, Jr.

freed from the idolatry and injustice of the Global Shopping Center gains authenticity from our behavior. We can anticipate in our own action something of what the new order would be like, for it is clear that in a just global society 6 percent of the people cannot continue to consume between 30 percent and 40 percent of the world's increasingly scarce resources of food and energy.

4. *Personal freedom.* The move toward simpler living can finally be seen as "an *act of self-defense* against the mind- and body-polluting effects of over-consumption" and as "an *act of withdrawal* from the achievement-neurosis of our high-pressure, materialist societies."[6] It is a declaration of independence from the magic spell Madison Avenue opportunists would cast over us, luring us with a life of ease and plenty, if only we leave all the decisions to them. The magic words that break the spell are a quiet but forceful "No, thank you" in reply to their constant and often frenzied propaganda. In fulfillment of Jesus' promise that those who lose their lives will find them, we discover that in taking concrete steps toward more responsible levels of consumption we regain control of our lives, winning freedom from the mental pollution and mind control that are part of the consumer treadmill.

One of the concrete steps we can take is to *change the way we talk* about our economic situation. How we talk affects what we think and feel. Too much poortalk sours our thinking and spoils our enjoyment of life. Thus, one action that all of us can profitably take is to alter our conversational patterns. We can *cut the poortalk,* and by so doing gain a truer perspective on our own situation. Consider some practical examples of how middle-class people might cut the poortalk:

"I *need* that" could become "I *want* that."

"I am underpaid" could become "I spend more than I make."

"I am poor" could become "My wants exceed my income." And perhaps the most familiar middle-class statement of all, "I can't afford it," could become "I choose to spend my money on other things." This last example acknowledges the fact that most of us *could* afford almost any reasonable item, *if* we made it a top priority. The fact is, we have other priorities on which we choose to spend our limited income. The choice is ours.

Simpler living is not easy, and it involves more than just changing the way we talk. It involves the breaking of long-established habits, strongly supported by our social environment. This is painful. At the same time it is joyful, for it involves celebration, the blessedness of giving—which exceeds that of receiving (Acts

20:35)—the integrity of authentic witness, and the regaining of personal freedom. Since joys are doubled and sorrows halved when they are shared, the path toward simpler living is one we need to walk with others. Members of families need to undertake the effort together, and single people need to find some "family" with whom to work. Elaine Amerson, who with her husband and two children lives and works with the poor in Evansville, Indiana, offers the following guidelines "for a family beginning to be aware of a need to simplify its lifestyle." Her first five suggestions deal with the need to learn from the Scriptures about God's concern for the poor and about the reality of poverty in our own community and worldwide. She then continues:

> 6. Plan strategies as a family and then take a first step toward simplification. Then take another—and another. Don't expect change to occur overnight; patterns weren't established quickly and won't be broken instantly either.
>
> 7. Emphasize the joyful life. Don't go on a "guilt trip." Look for ways to make the journey fun.
>
> 8. Talk with others who are attempting to simplify their lifestyles. Read books and magazines that will keep you in touch with such persons and ideas.
>
> 9. Become creative with interaction times, both as a family and with other families, persons, and groups.
>
> 10. Celebrate your successes.[7]

Point six is particularly important. While some have successfully adopted a "cold turkey" strategy, Elaine's slow-but-steady philosophy is likely to be more fruitful for most people. But where do we begin?

Our diets may be the best place. Everything comes together here. There may be no place where inflation is more visible than in the weekly trip to the supermarket. At the same time, our overconsumption of food and the desperate needs of a hungry world are becoming increasingly clear. One mother describes her family's efforts this way:

> We fight the junk-food battle constantly (and we win some and lose some), avoid processed foods and try to limit intake. We've joined a food cooperative, and we eat lots of soup and few desserts. We have also tried meat cutbacks, substituting alternative protein sources lower on the food chain. About twice a week I try to serve a delectable and colorful meatless meal. One evening I enthusiastically presented . . . a gourmet delight—zucchini soufflé. Our seven-year-old son sniffed and poked at his portion while I cheerily asked if someone could explain why we were having a meatless meal. Said he, with a heavy sigh, "Cause this is what the poor people have to eat?"[8]

An indispensable resource to many families trying to simplify their diets is Doris Longacre's *More-With-Less* cookbook.

Where next?

Transportation. Fewer cars? Smaller cars? More bikes and walking? Bus or subway?

Clothing. Do we depend on an artificial image? Do we need to let "them" dictate new purchases by arbitrary style changes? Secondhand shops?

Housing. Do we truly need all the house we can, in traditional terms, afford?

Leisure time, vacations, entertainment. Does genuine rest and recreation really require all the expensive toys that luxury industries have made available to us?

Books. This comes too close to home for us. Next.

Heating. Lower thermostat, warmer clothes? Is air conditioning necessary?

There are surely other budget areas and other questions to be explored. These are only intended as samples. For more extended discussion of the biblical rationale for simpler living and practical suggestions for implementing it, we recommend:

Adam Daniel Finnerty, *No More Plastic Jesus* (the story of the Shakertown pledge)

Arthur G. Gish, *Beyond the Rat Race*

Ronald J. Sider, ed., *Living More Simply*

John V. Taylor, *Enough Is Enough*

Simple living need not be sloppy living. It need not be tacky or boorish, devoid of the uplifting power of art, music, and literature. Nor need it mean wearing bib overalls and flannel shirts from a secondhand clothing store. Rather, as we simplify our lives we should strive to enrich them further not with dollars but with beauty. But in this area of our budgets as well as in every area we need to ask: Do we really need to *own* something, to possess it totally, in order to appreciate its beauty or enjoy its benefits? If, for example, we made more frequent visits to museums or borrowed art objects from our local library, could this enrich our lives without depriving others of the benefits of those objects? Or, if we are concerned about supporting the work of artists, could we purchase and then donate art objects to our local library or contribute the purchase price to a library or museum?

One final suggestion: It may look as if the exhaustion of the consumer treadmill is being traded in for the exhaustion of having to ask with every purchase, "Do we really need it?" There is an easy way to avoid this. It is called the graduated tithe. Instead of setting aside 10 percent of its income for the work of the Lord, including helping the poor, a family can set a higher percentage. When this is paid out first, like withholding tax, there is no choice but to find a way to live on what is left. Instead of agonizing over every particular decision, the task is just to adjust the overall budget to the available resources. This method also has the advantage of leaving the choice of which budget categories are to be pruned up to each family's individual preference. Since each family's circumstances are unique, no single set of guidelines for simplifying would be appropriate for everyone.

If a family accepts the challenge of the graduated tithe, Elaine Amerson's slow-but-steady strategy is important. A small increase, successfully handled and celebrated, will encourage the family to try another increase and then, perhaps, another. The larger a family's income, the greater the increase that should be possible. In this way we can learn to give unto God as we give unto Caesar; i.e., the larger the income, the larger the *percentage* we give to God. There is, of course, one tremendous difference. In God's case it is voluntary. Instead of a fate or destiny over which we feel we have almost no control, it is an exercise of our freedom as God's grateful children. That is why there can be joy in giving until it really pinches or, to use an older but not outmoded terminology, in sacrificial giving.

Action Toward Changing Our World

As our knowledge of biblical and global reality increases and as we take steps to bring our life as consumers into greater conformity with the faith we profess, we will find ourselves increasingly out of tune with our society. Changing ourselves is not enough; we will want to change the world in which we live. We will see that public policy and the plight of the poor are intimately linked, and we will find our political priorities beginning to change. As one world hunger group has said, "Each year Congress routinely chops about $200 million or more from an amount that has originally been recommended by its committees for development aid. Thus, in one vote Congress can wipe out the value of all contributions for church relief agencies for an entire year. In church we give to relieve hunger. By our silence on public policy we lock people more deeply into hunger . . . . No matter what else we do, if we neglect public policy, hunger increases."[9]

What kinds of public policy issues have a bearing on poverty, on who gets to eat and who does not? On the domestic front, the

FIGURE 6.3. "It says here that the simple lifestyle is the latest fad in America."
Drawing by Albert A. Bell, Jr.

most obvious issues are those of agricultural and domestic
assistance policies. Internationally speaking, trade and aid policies
have an equally clear impact.

But other, less obvious connections are just as important. Does
our foreign policy support regimes that promote the interests of the
already wealthy elites in the poor countries of the world or those
committed to the progress of the needy? Exactly the same question
can be asked about the impact of our investments abroad, both
through multinational corporations and through such agencies as
the World Bank and the International Monetary Fund, in which we

have a large voice. Then there is the question of military spending that now consumes nearly one billion dollars worldwide per day—money that could be used to alleviate human misery. As former president Eisenhower said, " 'Every gun that is made, every warship launched, every rocket fired signifies, in the final sense, a theft from those who hunger and are not fed, those who are cold and are not clothed.' "[10]

Our local congressman sends out a questionnaire from time to time asking the constituents what their highest political priorities are. Prominent among the suggested candidates are items appealing to our economic self-interest: taxes, inflation, government regulation. Conspicuously absent are the themes that would emerge from trying to shape political life by the anti-materialism and justice principles. What would be the impact if increasing numbers of Christian constituents (of which there are many) would fill in the "Other" blank with the message that they were less interested in improving their already affluent positions than in working to deal with real poverty both at home and abroad?

This question immediately brings two other questions to mind: (1) What is the point of all this, since I am just one little voice crying in the wilderness? (2) How would I ever be knowledgeable enough to back up my beliefs with specific suggestions?

Let us consider the second question first. Fortunately there are organized groups of Christians whose reason for being is to solve just this problem. Through analysis of the issues they help us see the impact of political decisions that are being made on the neediest people here and overseas, and through newsletters they call their members' attention to which bills are under debate, which policies are being formed, and which government officials need to be contacted. Two such groups are BREAD FOR THE WORLD (32 Union Square East, New York, NY 10003) and IMPACT (110 Maryland Avenue, N.E., Washington, DC 20002). Standing on a broad ecumenical base, they seek to provide the tools for Christian citizenship grounded in neither a conservative nor a liberal political philosophy, but in the biblical principle of being as concerned about our neighbor's well-being as about our own.

Groups such as these provide one answer to the first question as well. Because they coordinate activities at the national, state, and congressional district levels, individuals who participate can be sure that their voice is not being raised alone. In the age of special interest lobbies, there is a great need for such lobbies on behalf of those who otherwise have little or no voice at all in the decisions that are sometimes quite literally matters of life and death for them.

However, there is an even more important answer to the question about the effectiveness of raising a lonely voice. Even though there are ways of joining with other Christians to raise a united voice, there is no guarantee that it will not be drowned out by larger and louder voices of self-interested groups (including, sadly, Christians who have given in to the "politics of resentment," seeking to pin the blame for our economic troubles on the poor at home and abroad). But Christ has called us to faithful obedience, not to success in the sense of effectiveness. In the process of feeding the hungry, Jesus and a nameless lad taught us the spirit that needs to pervade our political activity. In spite of Andrew's objection (". . . but what is that among so many?") the lad was willing to give his five loaves and two fish to Jesus and trust him for the rest; and Jesus fed the five thousand (John 6:1-14). If we could free ourselves from Andrew's calculating spirit and offer our political loaves and fish to Christ in childlike trust, perhaps we would see miracles in our own time as well. In any case, Jesus never asks that we do more than we can. But he does ask that we do no less. To offer to Christ the gift of our citizenship means simply that we put it in the service of *his* kingdom and its righteousness rather than our own kingdom and its security.

Action Toward Changing Our Church

One reason we are likely to find so much need for change in our individual and family lives is that our churches have not heard and proclaimed the gospel on these issues as faithfully as on some others. As we ponder the implications of the biblical principles, it will be clear that changes are needed not only in our political institutions but in our religious institutions as well. This will be true on at least three levels, each of which involves the principle that the Christian life cannot be lived privately. It is a corporate life.

Learning Activities

First, there is the twofold task of biblical and global learning that we see as the basis for lifestyle and lobbying activities. The church teaches through its preaching, through its liturgy, and through its various Christian education programs. These need to be examined to see whether they are faithful to the whole counsel of God; in particular, whether they are giving sufficient attention to teaching the biblical witness we have been calling the anti-materialism and justice principles. The task of the Christian education program of a church is not simply to get people into the church and to keep them there; it is to make them *disciples* of Christ, teaching them to observe all that Jesus commanded.

Lifestyle Changes

If the first avenue of changed behavior involves the Christian education committee of the local church, the second involves the parish life, stewardship, and property committees. Given the pressures of our society, no individual and no family can make significant lifestyle simplifications alone. Support and encouragement are absolutely essential. Helping to organize the sharing and support groups that are needed here can be a task of the parish life committee. Meanwhile the stewardship committee can try to keep the financial life of the congregation from degenerating into fund raising and bill paying by making it an act of worship and serious discipleship. Building on the work the Christian education committee is doing in teaching what the Bible has to say about wealth and poverty, the stewardship committee can challenge the congregation to tithing (and graduated tithing) as an act of obedient celebration, solidarity with the poor, authentic witness, and personal freedom. Finally, the property committee (together with the stewardship committee) can take a long, hard look at the church's own corporate lifestyle. How much of the church's budget consists of prestige expenditures, made for the purpose of keeping up with or ahead of the ecclesiastical Joneses? Where can the local congregation simplify its own lifestyle? Why does the church pay its utility bills first and its benevolences only if the budget is met, when it teaches its members to give to God first and not make his kingdom depend on what is left over at the end of the month?

Lobbying Activities

Bringing political activity to the congregational level raises theological and legal questions about the separation of church and state. These questions cannot be ignored. But there are other difficult questions that also need to be asked. Why are most congregations so much less squeamish about singing hymns of praise to America's greatness than they are about voicing prophetic criticism of America's lifestyle? How much of the church's political inactivity is the result of a desire to keep peace by avoiding controversial issues and by avoiding any challenge to the congregation's own economic comfort? Are there times when speaking out on matters of public policy is not a matter of partisan

politics but of Christian principle? It might well be the task of the
Christian action or social justice committee to grapple with these
questions. Whatever answers the committee gives, it will be
important to keep in mind that corporate action is not the only way a
congregation can be politically involved. Just as it can provide a
fellowship of support for lifestyle changes that occur primarily at the
individual and family levels, so it can provide a context of
encouragement for personal political activity. It can organize local
chapters of groups like Bread for the World and Impact. It can hold
a "town meeting" type forum between the congregation and
candidates for public office.

No doubt few churches have exactly the committee structure
presupposed by the preceding paragraphs. We do not know any that
does. But that is not the point. We have two reasons for talking
about congregational change in terms of its committee structure.
First, a congregation's concern to be more just and less materialistic
needs to become "institutionalized." For all their problems,
institutional structures are the only way to give relative permanence
to a group's shared values. Second, the laity need to take the lead in
these matters. Most of our clergy have had little or nothing in their
seminary training to prepare them for prophetic leadership, and
their political instincts often encourage them not to rock the boat.
But if parishioners show they are willing to take the initiative, many
pastors will prove to be invaluable resources.

In moments when it all seems a bit overwhelming, think about
the Eastminster Presbyterian Church in Wichita, Kansas. They had
a $525,000 building program under way when Guatemala was
devastated by an earthquake in early 1976. At a meeting of their
board a lay person asked, " 'How can we set out to buy an
ecclesiastical Cadillac when our brothers and sisters in Guatemala
have just lost their little Volkswagen?' " After discussion the board
took two bold steps. First, they reduced their own building program
to $180,000, and then they sent their pastor and two elders to
Guatemala to look for ways to help. Based on their report, the
congregation borrowed $120,000 from a bank and with it rebuilt
twenty-six churches and twenty-eight parsonages for the Christians
in Guatemala. The Kansas church has kept in close contact with the
Guatemalan church and recently pledged another $40,000 for a new
seminary there. No doubt this has encouraged the church in
Guatemala. But the pastor in Kansas insists that it has "meant far
more to Eastminster Presbyterian than to Guatemala," and he talks
enthusiastically about the spiritual revitalization of his own

congregation.[11] The gospel *is* good news—if we only believe it.

Questions for Further Consideration

1. Can you illustrate from your own experience the way behavior shapes attitudes (for better or worse)?
2. What do you know about poverty in your own community? What contacts have you had with poor people?
3. Outside of your own family circle, what experiences have you had of the joy of sharing?
4. What practical steps could we take towards declaring our independence from the magic spell of Madison Avenue?
5. What lifestyle changes would be hardest for you? Which would be easiest? Does everyone need to make the same changes?
6. How could your church modify its own lifestyle and exert political leadership? ·

Looking to the Future

Part 3

7

What Is
Ahead for Us?

Predicting the future is risky business. Our national and global economies are so complex that economists have enough difficulty understanding and interpreting past events, let alone projecting future events. Changes in government policy, changes in international relations, changes in consumer attitudes and lifestyles all can occur rapidly enough to throw off even the most carefully plotted trend. Detroit's low projections for small-car sales in the late 1970s were based on car buyers' past preferences; the nation changed its preferences faster than the automakers could retool their products. Errors in crystal gazing are not restricted to business. In 1977, intelligence experts predicted that the Shah would rule Iran for at least ten more years.

But in spite of the difficulties in projecting the future, predictions continue to be made. Economists are more willing to speculate about the short-term future, since the forces that have already been set in motion will roll along on their own inertia for the next few years, barring revolutionary changes in our economy. Most economists agree that the cost of oil and petroleum products will continue to increase, that the productivity problem will not disappear overnight, and that high inflation will continue well into the mid-1980s.

No one predicts that the next few years will be easy. The transition to new sources of energy, the reversal of the productivity slide, and the continuing struggle with high inflation will strain our optimism. But then, what next? Is a new golden age of prosperity around the corner, or are we on the edge of a gaping abyss that will swallow our future? No one knows for sure, but both optimists and doomsayers can point to evidence supporting their point of view.

Let us take a look at two very different visions of the future in order to ponder the implications of those contrasting scenarios for Christian faith and life.

Scenario One: Unbounded Prosperity

Some people believe our problems have almost run their course. Each of the problems—high inflation, bulging unemployment lines, low consumer confidence, slumps in productivity, shortages of energy and raw materials—has faced our nation in earlier years. None of these crises has been sufficient to derail our economic engine. Instead, we moved out of each of these economic cycles with new resources, new technology to use those resources, new knowledge of economic principles, and new confidence in our ability to use both the knowledge and the technology wisely. A classic example of the flexibility of the world economy comes from the late 1800s. Supply problems had produced a critical shortage in the chief liquid fuel, whale oil. The situation looked extremely bleak, but the development of kerosene as an alternative fuel changed the course of economic history.

Is Continuous Prosperity Possible?

The optimists assert that our economy has a deep underlying strength that comes from a large, highly educated population of workers, a vast continent filled with natural resources, and millions of consumers accustomed to affluence. Our situation is certainly enviable compared to most other nations.

The American industry has long had a reputation for innovation and technological sophistication. Although recently a few nations have caught up with and surpassed us in certain areas of technology, our colleges and universities are pumping out young scientists and engineers who will design the next generation of equipment. While it is true that some of our resources are being depleted, the optimists are not worried. Our future prosperity does not depend on our estimated reserves of currently important natural resources, but rather on American ingenuity. Economist Julian Simon argues,

> . . . because we find new lodes, invent better production methods, and discover new substitutes, the ultimate constraint upon our capacity to enjoy unlimited raw materials at acceptable prices is knowledge. And the souce of knowledge is the human mind. Ultimately, then, the key constraint is human imagination and the exercise of educated skills.[1]

From this perspective, continued growth in affluence is not only possible but also increasingly likely as we discover more about nature and how to control it.

What Would the Future Be Like?

The year is 2010. The world's population has grown 50 percent since 1980. Almost six billion people are alive today, but the threats of widespread famine have not materialized. New farming technologies and the increased use of fertilizer have allowed farmers to keep up with the rising demand for grain, while biological discoveries have spawned a new "ocean farming" industry that now satisfies a major chunk of the world's protein needs.

Global per capita income has more than doubled since 1980, but the distribution of wealth is changing more slowly. For every $10,000 earned by a family in America or western Europe, a family in Black Africa or South Asia still receives less than $300.

Oil production has dropped steadily since the 1970s, but no one worries about it anymore. Energy is plentiful now (thanks mostly to the development of new, safer nuclear reactors using the fusion principle); so oil has become irrelevant as a fuel. Almost all the oil produced goes into fertilizer, and even there its use may soon be replaced by microorganisms that can turn municipal wastes into high quality fertilizer.

Here in the United States things have never been better. It is true that an economy car now costs $94,000; but since it is electric the fuel costs are low, and the hardened plastic body makes the exterior as maintenance-free as the engine. A modest home costs $250,000; but since the average family's annual income is $160,000, housing is actually more affordable than it was at any time in the past fifty years.

Our prosperity has grown steadily since the dark days of the early 1980s. It is true that we have had to give up a few things, such as long-distance vacations in the car, but everyone seems happy with the rise in our standard of living. Our values have not changed all that much; we still want the best and lots of it. But we Americans have also grown more sensitive to the needs of the poor around the world. For one thing, there are many more poor people than in 1980, since recent population growth has been entirely restricted to the less developed countries. But we also know more now about how to work together with the "newly rich" countries to help less developed nations stand on their own.

Looking back on it now, it seems that one key element in the success of the industrialized nations was our flexibility. When we ran out of one resource, we found something else that worked even better. For example, when we ran short of copper, we developed a fleet of communications satellites that eliminated the need for billions of miles of copper telephone lines. Another important element was our willingness to share some of our bounty with those less fortunate. That is the only way we could have weathered those food shortages without provoking a global confrontation between the rich and the poor. But now that food production has resumed its upward climb, and the world population is beginning to stabilize, the future for humanity once again looks bright.

How Might Christians Respond?

We hear the call of our Lord in times of prosperity as well as in times of adversity. But it is clear that there are dangers involved in an era of unchecked growth in prosperity. Affluent Christians run the risk of casting aside the anti-materialism principle, putting money and possessions rather than God at the center of our lives. This grasping greediness—what Philip Slater calls "wealth addiction"—was traditionally regarded as one of the seven deadly sins.[2] It is dangerous not only because it can undermine our personal adjustment, but also because it threatens to evoke God's judgment for our rebellion against his commands. The greed that makes us pile up possessions is really a demonstration of our "unfaith," our lack of trust in God's ability to meet our needs.

Christians also face the temptation to ignore the justice principle. We turn away from pictures of starving children and avoid the shrill clamor of prophetic voices from inside and outside the church, because it is somehow easier to enjoy our affluence if we can forget about those who do not share it. We can become so entwined in our own luxury that we hear the anguished cries of the suffering as threats to our lifestyle rather than as pleas for help.

Yet the troubling questions refuse to go away. To what degree has our prosperity depended upon colonial relationships with the rest of the world? What have we given the poor countries in return for using their resources and their labor? Are some people starving so that we might maintain our rising standard of living? These are controversial questions, but they raise an even more fundamental issue: Regardless of whether our wealth has been acquired by just or unjust means, by what right can we refuse to share our bounty?

Christians can guard themselves against the temptations of pride and greed and selfishness while still joyfully celebrating God's good gifts. Here are four suggestions for doing so:

1. We can continually acknowledge that God's goodness is the ultimate source of our prosperity.

2. We can serve as role models for Christians and non-Christians alike by demonstrating that lives of moderate consumption or "creative simplicity" are possible and desirable even in times of prosperity.

3. We can go out of our way to confront true poverty so that none of us forgets that economic justice has not yet prevailed.

4. We can join with other concerned individuals to urge governments and other institutions to work toward alleviating poverty and economic oppression throughout the world.

Scenario Two: Running Out of Everything

A growing chorus of environmentalists, economists, and scientists is challenging the assumptions of the previous scenario. Rather than seeing our current problems as temporary fluctuations in our long-term upward climb, some of these doomsayers hail them as signs of the end of an era, the last gasps of a dying industrial society, poisoned by its own excesses.

For years, prophets of disaster have grabbed occasional headlines. But now respected, conscientious scientists and statesmen are adding their voices to the dire predictions. The possibility of worldwide disaster gained considerable credibility in 1980 with the publication of the Global 2000 Study, a report prepared by the United States Council on Environmental Quality and the United States State Department. The three-year study concluded:

> If present trends continue, the world in 2000 will be more crowded, more polluted, less stable ecologically, and more vulnerable to disruption than the world we live in now. Serious stresses involving population, resources, and environment are clearly visible ahead. Despite greater material output, the world's people will be poorer in many ways than they are today.
>
> For hundreds of millions of the desperately poor, the outlook for food and other necessities of life will be no better. For many it will be worse. Barring revolutionary advances in technology, life for most people on earth will be more precarious in 2000 than it is now—unless the nations of the world act decisively to alter current trends.[3]

Mouths to Feed

Even conservative estimates of population trends project a 50 percent increase by the turn of the century. The world's population will grow from four billion today to over six billion, with 92 percent of this growth occurring in the poorest countries. The earth certainly can hold six billion people, or even more, but these billions will not be distributed evenly across the habitable regions. The industrialized nations will grow by only 17 percent, while the populations of Africa and Latin America will double. Mexico City will burst at the seams with thirty million inhabitants, while Bombay and Calcutta will each reach twenty million.[4]

The income gap between rich and poor nations is projected to become even larger. For every twenty-dollar increase in per-person incomes in the industrialized countries, the less developed nations will receive only one dollar.[5] This means that the poorer countries will be even less able to pay for the projected doubling in food prices over the next two decades.

Why would food prices climb? In 1970, one hectare (about 2.5 acres) supported 2.6 persons; by 2000, one hectare will have to support 4 persons or even more if urban sprawl and erosion continue to nibble away at existing cropland.[6] This increase in food production would be possible only through the increased use of fertilizer and pesticides derived from oil. If oil prices rise, so will food costs. What is more, the increased use of fertilizer produces diminishing returns. Each extra pound of fertilizer produces fewer and fewer additional pounds of grain; at some point an additional pound of fertilizer would be required for each additional pound of grain (see Figure 7.1).

What about the oceans? Can we depend on their bounty to feed the extra mouths? Unfortunately, the world fish catch has probably reached its peak. Between 1969 and 1975 the world's fishing fleet grew by 50 percent, but the total fish catch did not increase at all.[7]

What about our technology? Will our scientific ingenuity ultimately solve our problems? Perhaps, but we seem to be reaching a point of diminishing returns in some technological investments as well as in agriculture. Each year it takes more and more worker-hours and more and more money to produce each important advance. For example, the millions of dollars spent on cancer research have not produced as many scientific break-throughs as comparable sums did in the past. What is more, some argue that technology could not possibly be the solution, since it is part of the problem. Our dilemmas over pollution and toxic waste disposal are by-products of our technological sophistication.

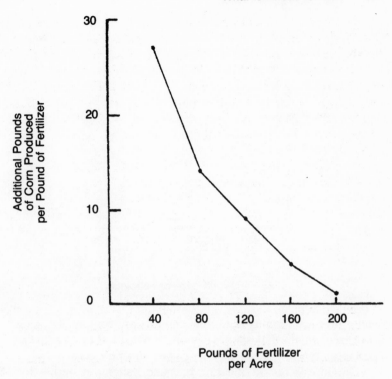

FIGURE 7.1. Diminishing returns in food production as fertilizer usage increases. Past increases in food production partly reflect increased fertilization. Further increases in fertilizer usage will produce less benefit. Thus, it is unlikely that per-acre yields will continue to grow as they have in the past.

Depleted Resources

One of the key elements in the rising prosperity of the western nations over the last century was cheap, readily available energy. The oil price hikes of the 1970s ended the era of cheap energy (see Figure 7.2) and spurred conservation efforts around the world. But many experts believe that we have already used half of all the world's reserves of oil and that the remainder of the easily accessible oil will be depleted early in the next century. Alternative energy sources hold promise for the next century, but for the next twenty to thirty years we can expect energy to be less readily available and more costly.

Other important resources are also endangered. The world production of many minerals is falling. The easily accessible, high

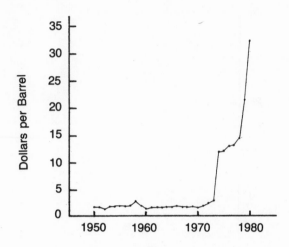

FIGURE 7.2. World price of petroleum.

quality ores are running out. New deposits are continually being discovered, but the deposits are in more remote locations, are lower in quality, and require more energy per unit produced.

Our forests provide heating fuel and building materials for most of the world's population, but demand for wood has increased faster than trees can be planted. By one estimate, 40 percent of the existing forests in less developed countries will have disappeared by the turn of the century.[8] This and other strains on the air, the water, and the delicate balance of our fragile biosphere could make the earth much less hospitable to its human inhabitants.

What Would the Future Be Like?

The year is 2010. The earth is teeming with life; more people are alive today than ever before—more than twice as many as there were just half a century ago. Yet the earth is dying a slow death from a thousand wounds.

Hundreds of millions of its inhabitants are starving, and millions more will suffer lifelong physical and intellectual retardation from insufficient protein. Once-fertile farms and grasslands are dry and barren; each year an area the size of Maine has succumbed to the encroaching desert, helped along by overgrazing and overcultivating.

Huge tracts of forest have vanished. Nearly 20 percent of all the animal species alive in 1980 are now extinct—starved by the loss of their forest-based food supply or poisoned by the steady buildup of toxic wastes in the environment.

Here in the United States we have been relatively sheltered from the worst effects of the global crisis. We have plenty to eat, even though beef has disappeared from the tables of everyone except the very wealthy. Our diets are well balanced; but they do not have as much variety as in the past since shipping costs have pushed out-of-season vegetables and fruits out of our reach.

Our prosperity has declined quite a bit from its peak in the late 1970s, but life in the United States is still good, especially considering the misery in so many other places. Sure, we have got some problems—decaying cities, polluted streams, high prices for everything—but we'll survive. The worst part is the heat. The experts claim that air pollution plus the loss of the forests in other countries have created a chemical "greenhouse" around the earth, and it is getting hotter all the time. And now that air conditioners have been outlawed, you can imagine how we are suffering.

But most of us have good jobs, at least for now. The outlook for the future is less cheery. The news reports say that shortages in raw materials and energy will close a lot of factories and that people will be forced to move back onto the farms.

Looking back on it now, I am not sure that anything we could have done would have saved those animals or fed those starving children or kept me as well off as I was thirty years ago. But I wish someone would have told us what was in store for us so that at least we could have been prepared.

How Might Christians Respond to This Dismal Scenario?

Clearly the world faces some serious challenges stemming from the *physical limits* of our resources in the next decades, even if no *social limits* develop. In the event of wars, revolutions, or economic conflicts between rich and poor countries, even the scenario just described could turn out to be naively optimistic. Not only would millions starve in the poorer nations, but even rich Americans could see their standard of living collapse.

Proverbs 30:8 says, ". . . give me neither poverty nor wealth . . . . " It is easy to see the dangers of affluence. The dangers of poverty may be less obvious, but they are equally serious. Poor Christians risk falling into a depression not of the economy but of the spirit. This hopelessness is dangerous, because it is really a symptom of an even more basic problem: the loss of trust in God's providence. Some Christians caught in this trap may give up on the world and turn to an otherworldly hope as an escape from the miseries of this life. Other Christians who have lost faith in God's ability or willingness to sustain them may become even more materialistic, putting their survival in the hands of their possessions rather than in God.

The first of these responses denies the goodness of creation, while the second denies the goodness of the Creator. Both ignore the justice principle; Christians who turn inward, either to escape their problems or satisfy their materialism, will be less likely to share what they have with others.

But impoverished Christians can guard themselves from the traps of despair and escapism while still celebrating God's good gifts. Here are four suggestions for doing so:

1. We can seriously consider the possibility that our individual, national, or global economic problems could be God's judgment on wayward people, rather than evidence of God's powerlessness.

2. We can use our forced separation from material luxuries as an opportunity to cultivate a healthy spirituality and rediscover life's ultimate meaning.

3. We can still go out of our way to come in contact with those who are even less fortunate than we are.

4. We can join forces with other individuals to work for economic justice in business, in government, and in society's other institutions.

Questions for Further Consideration

1. How optimistic are you about our economic future? Which of the scenarios seems most realistic? Why?
2. Each generation of Americans has worked hard to ensure a better life for its children. Do you think that your children will be better or worse off than you are? How would you feel if your children had to settle for less than you have?
3. Who would we blame if the dismal scenario comes about? Who would get the credit if our prosperity continues to grow? Who should get the credit?
4. Some people have argued for "lifeboat ethics." That is, in order to protect the future of the world, we will need to "throw

overboard" some of the countries that have few resources but increasing numbers of hungry mouths. If we do not, they argue, we will all sink together. What do you think?

5. Is it harder to live as a Christian in times of prosperity than in times of adversity? Why or why not?

8

Seeing the Light Through Inflation's Gloom

Every old sailor has a favorite story about the wild storms at sea, where the ships drop so deeply into each wave's valley that the sailors lose sight of both where they are going and from where they have come. For a long moment the world consists of nothing more than the water swirling around the decks, until at last the lighthouse beacon appears over the crest of the wave.

Today's Americans are a lot like those sailors: We measure our lives not by where we have been or where we are going, but by how we are doing compared to last year or even last month. We have a chronically short-term perspective. We see the economy swirling around our heads, but we are so mesmerized by its every dip and flutter that we are unable to see the years of blessings stretching out behind us or the opportunities and challenges that lie ahead of us.

One of our goals in this book has been to call attention to the broader perspective—to see the light beaming through inflation's swirling gloom. The light we see comes not from a "pot of gold" at the end of inflation's rainbow, nor from a "pie-in-the-sky" vision of a future utopia. Rather, the source of our light is God's promise: Through the person and work of Jesus Christ, God has set in motion the redemption not only of individual persons but also of his entire creation, including the economic and social systems that control distribution of material goods.

That means our reactions to the economic situation can be informed by our Christian faith. Faith provides both the motivation for change and the criterion to guide the changes. It also provides us with hope. By faith we are profoundly optimistic about the future, first because we are confident that God's kingdom will ultimately prevail and secondly because he has made us partners in the victory.

But we are not blind. We live in a world that has been redeemed; yet evil persists. We worship in a church filled with saints who are yet sinners. There is a constant tension between the "already" and the "not yet," between the present beginnings and the future fulfillments.

The invasion of Normandy in 1944 was a turning point in World War II. In that one swift blow the Allies had "won the war." They had broken the backbone of the enemy, and victory was assured. The war was over—yet the killing went on. Likewise, God's kingdom of righteousness and justice has already invaded our world, and victory is already assured. Yet the full reality of the kingdom is still to come.

But we do not have to wait for this final victory before we begin to change our attitudes, our lives, and our world. If what we are hoping for is God's kingdom of justice and peace, then we ought to be working now for justice and peace in this world. As Jurgen Moltmann asserts, "Peace with God means conflict with the world, for the goad of the promised future stabs inexorably into the flesh of every unfulfilled present." [1]

From this perspective, the failures of our present economic and social systems are not a cause for despair but an invitation for action. We can make a difference! Carl Braaten puts it this way: Those who catch a vision of the future kingdom are like advance explorers, dashing ahead, but then coming back to lead the way. [2] This image of hope refuses to allow us to be content with the present; it incites us to begin the journey and gives comfort and encouragement when the way becomes difficult.

Thus Martin Luther King could declare, "I have a dream." His dream was an eschatological hope that explodes into the present, penetrating every aspect of our existence and breaking down the barriers to the promised future. For those who catch the vision of the future age, it has begun already. It has begun among those who have linked life and destiny with Jesus Christ. "When anyone is united to Christ," writes Paul, "there is a new act of creation; the old order has gone, and a new order has already begun" (2 Corinthians 5:17, alternate reading).

This vision of a world liberated from economic injustice, oppression, and suffering is a vision that directs and gives hope to our work here on earth. To paraphrase Rubem Alves, the melody of the promised future enables us to dance even now. [3]

Questions for Further Consideration

1. Why are people today so shortsighted? Is it because of the rapid changes in our society? Our disinterest in history? The media? Or other factors?
2. In view of the dismal predictions that some have made, how can Christians be optimistic about the future?
3. Can you think of any concrete examples in which a vision of hope compelled people to keep working in spite of difficult and discouraging circumstances?
4. Has this book changed your perspective on wealth or your attitudes toward your own economic situation? If so, how? And what are you going to do about it?

Notes

Chapter 1

[1]The figures in this section were computed by the Tax Foundation, a nonprofit research group with headquarters in Washington, D.C.

[2]Average annual benefits rose from $1,021 in 1967 to $3,144 in 1978. However, supplemental retirement income from private sources has risen much more slowly. Therefore, Social Security increases may have simply kept total retirement incomes from shrinking.

[3]"Inflation Is Wrecking the Private Pension System," *Business Week* (May 12, 1980), p. 99.

[4]The lagging wages of librarians, secretaries, and other traditionally female occupations illustrate the problem faced by families headed by single working mothers. And benefits through Aid to Dependent Children have also failed to keep up with inflation, falling in real value by 20 percent between 1970 and 1977.

[5]Joseph J. Minarik, "Who Wins, Who Loses from Inflation?" *Challenge,* vol. 21, no. 6 (January/February, 1979), pp. 26-31.

[6]See Lester C. Thurow, *The Zero-Sum Society* (New York: Basic Books, Inc., Publishers, 1980).

[7]Fred Hechinger, "Schoolyard Blues: The Decline of Public Education," *Saturday Review,* vol. 6 (January 20, 1979), p. 22.

[8]Some economists claim that the real problem of inflation arises only when it is unanticipated. To counter this, some countries, such as Israel and Brazil, have introduced widespread indexing of all wages, contracts, debts, and taxes to the rate of inflation. The results have not been entirely satisfactory, however, since such systems tend to build in further upward bias to prices, causing them to spiral upward even faster. Furthermore, even with indexing, sellers have to use up real resources just to change price tags more often, and buyers have to use up more shoe leather and nervous energy trying to comparative shop before the next round of price increases outdates their findings.

[9]See Joseph Peckman and Emil Sunley, "Inflation Adjustment for Individual Income Tax," in *Inflation and the Income Tax,* ed. Henry J. Aaron (Washington, D.C.: The Brookings Institution, 1976).

[10]Technically speaking, since most sales taxes and property taxes are set as a constant proportion of the item's value, in one sense the "burden" of the tax cannot be said to increase unless an increase in tax rates is voted. But since an increase in the value of an item such as a home may not correspond with the person's ability to pay a higher tax on it, the "burden" of a tax may actually increase without an increase in tax rates.

[11]Avraham Shama, "Thomas Hobbes, Meet Howard Jarvis: The Impact of Stagflation on Society," *Public Opinion* (November/December, 1978), pp. 56-9.

[12]See Richard T. Curtin, "Social-Psychological Impact of Stagflation: An Overview" (Paper presented to the American Psychological Association, 1979).

[13]F. Harvey Popell, "How Inflation Undermines Morality," *Business Week* (May 5, 1980), p. 20.

Chapter 2

[1]Lance Morrow, "Epitaph for a Decade," *Time*, vol. 115, no. 1 (January 7, 1980), p. 38.

[2]Total taxes per capita in the United States are also relatively low: $2,200 in this country, compared to $2,700 in Germany and $4,595 in Sweden for 1976.

[3]It is possible that the *way* taxes are collected and benefits paid may adversely affect output by discouraging additional effort. Some workers may refuse overtime because the double effect of more income and more inflation would push them into a higher tax bracket, leaving them no better off—or even worse—than before. Also, an unemployed worker receiving unemployment benefits nearly equivalent to full pay may refuse alternative employment at a wage lower than benefits received.

[4]Deficit spending is not new. Throughout history the most bitter condemnations have been made of those sovereigns who debased the currency in order to pay for royal expenditures. Citizens were outraged to find the few coins in their savings (which had been accumulated in order to expand business or provide for old age) suddenly worth half their face value, simply because the king needed money to wage a war. It was worse than usury, because at least in the latter case the borrower voluntarily agreed to pay interest on the loan; not so when the king financed a war with inflation.

[5]By some measures, productivity actually fell in the latter half of the 1970s.

[6]Some price increases, of course, result from "profit-push" by producers not facing stiff competition.

[7]However, in 1978 electric utilities and the petroleum industry spent a larger share (9 percent) of their investment funds on pollution abatement. Together their expenditures accounted for two-thirds of all spending to meet environmental standards. Interestingly, they are the industries for which productivity declines in recent years have been greatest.

[8]However, improvements have recently been made in the efficiency of environmental protection. Now that the competitive market has been harnessed (via tax incentives and penalties) to produce a greater array of cost-effective pollution-control methods, one drag on productivity growth may have been reduced.

[9]Alfred L. Malabre, Jr., "Living-Standard Gauge Shows Big Rise Since Carter Became President," *The Wall Street Journal* (December 2, 1980), p. 56.

Chapter 3

[1]From Burkhard Strumpel, "Economic Lifestyles, Values, and Subjective Welfare," in *Economic Means for Human Needs,* ed. Burkhard Strumpel (Ann Arbor: University of Michigan Survey Research Center, 1976), pp. 19-65.

[2]David Myers and Thomas Ludwig, "Let's Cut the Poortalk," *Saturday Review,* vol. 5, no. 27 (October 28, 1978), p. 24. The remainder of the discussion in chapter 3 is based on this article. Other footnoted material in this chapter serves as elaboration on the principle discussion.

[3]Philip Brickman and Donald T. Campbell, "Hedonic Relativism and Planning the Good Society," in *Adaptation-Level Theory,* ed. M. H. Appley (New York: Academic Press, 1971), p. 287.

[4]See George H. Gallup, "Human Needs and Satisfactions: A Global Survey,"

The Public Opinion Quarterly, vol. 40, no. 4 (Winter, 1976-1977), pp. 459-67.

[5]Philip Brickman, Dan Coates, and Ronnie Janoff-Bulman, "Lottery Winners and Accident Victims: Is Happiness Relative?" *Journal of Personality and Social Psychology,* vol. 36, no. 8 (August, 1978), pp. 917-27.

[6]From George Katona, "Persistence of Belief in Personal Financial Progress," in *Economic Means for Human Needs,* ed. Burkhard Strumpel (Ann Arbor: University of Michigan Survey Research Center, 1976), pp. 83-105.

[7]For a review of this concept, see Faye Crosby, "A Model of Egoistical Relative Deprivation," *Psychological Review,* vol. 83, no. 2 (1976), pp. 85-113.

[8]*Ibid.,* p. 85.

[9]*Ibid.,* p. 85.

[10]*Ibid.,* p. 86.

[11]Brickman and Campbell, *op. cit.,* p. 296.

[12]For a review of this concept, see David G. Myers, *The Inflated Self: Human Illusions and the Biblical Call to Hope* (New York: The Seabury Press, Inc., 1980).

[13]*Ibid.,* pp. 23-4.

[14]B. R. Schlenker and R. S. Miller, "Egocentrism in Groups: Self-Serving Biases or Logical Information Processing?" *Journal of Personality and Social Psychology,* vol. 35, no. 10 (October, 1977), pp. 755-64.

[15]"Why Do Consumers Fear Inflation?" *Institute for Social Research Newsletter* (Spring, 1979), p. 6. The *ISR Newsletter* is edited by Douglas Truax and is available from the University of Michigan, Institute for Social Research, Box 1248, Ann Arbor, MI 48106.

[16]Samuel A. Stouffer *et. al., The American Soldier: Adjustment During Army Life,* vol. 1 (Princeton, N.J.: Princeton University Press, 1949), pp. 250-3.

[17]Crosby, *op. cit.,* p. 86.

Chapter 4

[1]Merold Westphal, "Kierkegaard's Politics," *Thought,* vol. 55 (September, 1980), pp. 320-32.

[2]See Henry Fairlie, *The Seven Deadly Sins Today* (Notre Dame, Ind.: University of Notre Dame Press, 1979); and Stanford Lyman, *The Seven Deadly Sins* (New York: St. Martin's Press, Inc., 1978).

[3]From Plato's *Republic* (trans. Benjamin Jowett), bk. 2.

[4]Could Jesus have had in mind Proverbs 14:31, "He who oppresses the poor insults his Maker; he who is generous to the needy honours him," or Proverbs 19:17, "He who is generous to the poor lends to the LORD"?

[5]For more detailed discussion of these laws see Ronald J. Sider, *Rich Christians in an Age of Hunger* (Downers Grove, Ill.: Inter-Varsity Press, 1977), chapter 4; and John V. Taylor, *Enough Is Enough* (Minneapolis: Augsburg Publishing House, 1975), chapter 3.

[6]The word translated "gain" at the end of this passage in the NEB is the Hebrew *betsa.* It is a very strong word for greed. Taylor, *op. cit.,* pp. 43-4.

[7]In *Rich Christians* (p. 131) Ron Sider tells of the time Upton Sinclair read this passage (James 5:1-7) to a group of ministers, attributing it to a contemporary anarchist agitator. Their response was to call for the woman's deportation, not recognizing the passage as part of the Bible.

[8]Adam Daniel Finnerty, *No More Plastic Jesus* (Maryknoll, N.Y.: Orbis Books, 1977), p. 70. See also Barnet and Muller, *Global Reach* (New York: Simon and Schuster, Inc., 1975); and Pierro Gheddo, *Why Is the Third World Poor?* trans. Kathryn Sullivan (Maryknoll, N.Y.: Orbis Books, 1973).

[9]Sider, *op. cit.,* pp. 127-8.

[10]On the nature and significance of the practice of Jesus and the disciples in this regard, see the RCA General Synod statement, "Holy Living in Time of Famine," *Church Herald* (August 8, 1975), p. 6.

[11]Our concept of fellowship reflects the New Testament understanding of "koinonia" much less fully than our notion of sharing. Paul uses the term to refer to economic as well as spiritual sharing.

Chapter 5

[1]Quoted in E. F. Schumacher, "Small Is Beautiful: Toward a Theology of 'Enough'," *The Christian Century* (July 28, 1971), p. 901.

[2]"Pater-$-familias," *New York Times* (November 4, 1979), sec. 4, p. E-21.

[3]In a letter to the editor of the *New York Times* (November 17, 1979), C. L. Hardin responds: "Actually, it's rather comforting to find that at least one of the deadly sins—greed—can on occasion be self-punishing."

[4]A prime example of this line of argument can be found in Dr. Chauncey Starrs' keynote address to the Symposium on Science, Technology, and the Human Prospect in San Francisco (April, 1979).

[5]See Carl E. Braaten, "Caring for the Future: Where Ethics and Ecology Meet," in *Eschatology and Ethics,* ed. Carl E. Braaten (Minneapolis: Augsburg Publishing House, 1974).

[6]From Burkhard Strumpel, "Economic Lifestyles, Values, and Subjective Welfare," in *Economic Means for Human Needs,* ed. Burkhard Strumpel (Ann Arbor: University of Michigan Survey Research Center, 1976), pp. 19-65.

[7]Philip Brickman and Donald T. Campbell, "Hedonic Relativism and Planning the Good Society," in *Adaptation-Level Theory,* ed. M. H. Appley (New York: Academic Press, 1971), p. 287.

[8]See Matthew 5 in *The Interpreter's Bible,* G. A. Buttrick, gen. ed. (Nashville: Abingdon Press, 1951), vol. 7.

[9]See Melvin J. Lerner, *The Belief in a Just World* (New York: Plenum Publishing Corporation, 1980).

[10]Tom Minnery, "Wealth 'Never Seems to Be Enough', " *Mesquite Daily News,* Dallas, Texas, in *Leadership,* vol. 1, no. 3 (Summer, 1980), p. 46. Reprinted with permission.

[11]Bertha G. Maslow, ed., *Abraham H. Maslow: A Memorial Volume* (Monterey, Calif.: Brooks/Cole Publishing Company, 1972), p. 108.

[12]Marshall Dermer *et al.,* "Evaluative Judgments of Aspects of Life as a Function of Vicarious Exposure to Hedonic Extremes," *Journal of Personality and Social Psychology,* vol. 37, no. 2 (February, 1979), pp. 247-60.

Chapter 6

[1]See David G. Myers, *The Human Puzzle* (New York: Harper and Row, Publishers, Inc., 1978), chapters 5 and 6, especially pp. 100-2.

[2]From the filmstrip *Hunger and Public Policy.* Available from Bread for the World, 32 Union Square East, New York, NY 10003.

[3]You can meet Pitung in Adam Daniel Finnerty's *No More Plastic Jesus* (Maryknoll, N.Y.: Orbis Books, 1977), pp. 12-3; José in Judy Alexander's "José Is Angry," *The Other Side,* vol. 13, no. 8 (December, 1977), pp. 45-7; and Alberto in the filmstrip *Guess Who's Coming to Breakfast,* available from Packard Manse Media Project, Box 450, Stoughton, MA 02072.

[4]*RCAgenda* (May/June, 1980), pp. 15-6. Copies of the *RCAgenda* can be ordered from the RCA Distribution Center, 18525 Torrence Avenue, Lansing, IL 60438.

[5]From page 5 of the paper "An Evangelical Commitment to Simple Lifestyle," issued in March, 1980, by an international consultation cosponsored by the Theology and Education Group of the Lausanne Committee on World Evangelization and the Unit on Ethics and Society of the World Evangelical Fellowship.

⁶Jorgen Lissner, "Ten Reasons for Choosing a Simpler Lifestyle," *How to Become a Poor Church (and Save Faith)*, p. 2. This publication was produced by the United Presbyterian Program Agency's Unit on Ministry with Congregations in cooperation with the Hunger Programs of the United Presbyterian Church in the U.S.A. and the Presbyterian Church in the United States.

⁷Ronald J. Sider, ed., *Living More Simply* (Downers Grove, Ill.: InterVarsity Press, 1980), pp. 66-7. © 1980 by Inter-Varsity Christian Fellowship of the USA and used by permission of InterVarsity Press.

⁸*Ibid.*, pp. 105-6.

⁹From the filmstrip *Hunger and Public Policy*.

¹⁰From the filmstrip *Hunger and Public Policy*.

¹¹Ronald J. Sider, "Cautions Against Ecclesiastical Elegance," *Christianity Today*, vol. 23, no. 20 (August 17, 1979), p. 14.

Chapter 7

¹Julian L. Simon, "Resources, Population, Environment: An Oversupply of False Bad News," *Science*, vol. 208 (June 27, 1980), p. 1436.

²Philip Slater, "Wealth Addiction," *Quest/77*, vol. 1, no. 5 (November/December, 1977), pp. 52-6, 108-9.

³The Council on Environmental Quality and the Department of State, Gerald O. Barney, study dir., *The Global 2000 Report to the President: Entering the Twenty-First Century*, vol. 1 (1980), p. 1. The complete report can be purchased from the Superintendent of Documents, U.S. Government Printing Office, Washington, DC 20402.

⁴*Ibid.*, pp. 8-9, 12.

⁵*Ibid.*, p. 13.

⁶*Ibid.*, p. 16.

⁷Lester R. Brown, "Global Economic Ills: The Worst May Be Yet to Come," *The Futurist*, vol. 12, no. 3, p. 158.

⁸*The Global 2000 Report*, vol. 1, *op. cit.*, p. 2.

Chapter 8

¹Jurgen Moltmann, *The Theology of Hope* (New York: Harper and Row, Publishers, Inc., 1976), p. 21.

²Carl E. Braaten, "The Significance of the Future: An Eschatological Perspective," in *Hope and the Future of Man*, new ed., ed. Evert Cousins (Philadelphia: Fortress Press, 1972), p. 44.

³Bruce C. Birch and Larry L. Rasmussen, *The Predicament of the Prosperous* (Philadelphia: The Westminster Press, 1978), p. 145.

Sources of Charts and Graphs

FIGURE 1.1. U.S. Bureau of the Census, *Statistical Abstract of the United States: 1980*, 101st ed. (Washington, D.C., 1980), p. 339.

FIGURE 1.2. Tax Foundation, Inc., *Facts and Figures on Government Finance*, 20th biennial ed. (Washington, D.C., 1979), p. 34.

FIGURE 2.1. Tax Foundation, Inc., *Facts and Figures on Government Finance*, 20th biennial ed. (Washington, D.C., 1979), p. 35.

FIGURE 2.2. U.S. Bureau of the Census, *Statistical Abstract of the United States: 1980*, 101st ed. (Washington, D.C., 1980), pp. 487-488. Earlier data from the 1940, 1950, 1960, and 1970 editions.

FIGURE 2.3. U.S. Bureau of the Census, *Historical Statistics of the United States, Colonial Times to 1970*, bicentennial ed., pt. 1 (Washington, D.C., 1975), p. 225.

FIGURE 2.4. *Saturday Review,* February 16, 1980, p. 8.

FIGURE 3.1. U.S. Bureau of the Census, *Historical Statistics of the United States, Colonial Times to 1970,* bicentennial ed., pt. 1 (Washington, D.C., 1975), p. 225; and "National Income and Product Accounts Tables," *Survey of Current Business,* vol. 61, no. 2 (February, 1981), pp. 5, 9. Earlier data from the February editions of 1974, 1976, 1978, and 1980.

FIGURE 3.2. Happiness data from Tom W. Smith, "Happiness: Time Trends, Seasonal Variations, Intersurvey Differences, and Other Mysteries," *Social Psychology Quarterly,* vol. 42 (1979), pp. 18-30. Income data from the U.S. Bureau of the Census, *Historical Statistics of the United States, Colonial Times to 1970,* bicentennial ed., pt. 1 (Washington, D.C., 1975), p. 225.

FIGURE 4.1. *The Church Herald,* June 29, 1979.

FIGURE 6.1. *Saturday Review,* September 2, 1978, p. 49.

FIGURE 7.1. Lester R. Brown, "Global Economic Ills: The Worst May Be Yet to Come," *The Futurist,* vol. 12, no. 3, pp. 156-168.

FIGURE 7.2. International Monetary Fund, *International Financial Statistics Yearbook* (Washington, D.C., 1980), pp. 80-81.

Index